# THE MONTY ALEXANDER COLLECTION

**Transcribed by**

BRUCE CAMERON MUNSON

**Cover photo by**

TERI BLOOM

ISBN 0-7935-6045-4

**HAL•LEONARD®**
**CORPORATION**
7777 W. BLUEMOUND RD. P.O. BOX 13819 MILWAUKEE, WI 53213

Visit Hal Leonard Online at
**www.halleonard.com**

# BIOGRAPHY

Monty Alexander was born in 1944 in Kingston, Jamaica. He began piano lessons at the age of six. As a teenager, he was often invited to sit in with the bands of some of the prominent local musicians. In addition, he had the opportunity to attend performances of Louis Armstrong and Nat 'King' Cole at the Carib theatre, and his style of playing was deeply influenced by their 'gospel of jazz.' He formed a band called Monty and the Cyclones, which recorded songs that charted on the Jamaican pop charts between 1958 and 1960.

He moved to Miami in 1961, and by 1963 was playing piano with Art Mooney's orchestra. Jilly Rizzo and Frank Sinatra heard him, and Monty was hired to play at Jilly's club in New York. There, he played solo and accompanied many well known personalities of the entertainment world, including Mr. Sinatra. It was at Jilly's that he met vibraharpist Milt Jackson, who hired Monty to join his group. Soon after, Monty began an association with bassist Ray Brown which lasted many years. He also performed with such jazz giants as Dizzy Gillespie, Clark Terry and Sonny Rollins.

Since 1964, Monty has become extremely active as a pianist and composer. He has recorded with Quincy Jones and was heard on the soundtrack of Clint Eastwood's movie *Bird* about the life of Charlie Parker. In 1991, he assisted Natalie Cole in the seven time grammy award winning album *Unforgettable*, a tribute to her father Nat. In 1993, he performed at Carnegie Hall in a tribute to the beloved pianist Erroll Garner.

From 1993 to 1995, Monty performed at the Montreux Jazz Festival in Switzerland - two years accompanying opera singer Barbara Hendricks in a program of Duke Ellington compositions, and in 1995 with an all-Jamaican reggae group. This performance was recorded for Island Records, and the CD is called *Yard Movement*. Monty performed Gershwin's "Rhapsody in Blue" with Bobby McFerrin conducting at the Verbier Festival in Switzerland in 1996.

Monty continues to be a much sought-after solo artist and accompanist, with over fifty CD's released under his own name. He presents music in several contexts: soloist, trio format, performances with big band or symphony orchestra, and a return to his Jamaican roots with the unique "groovin'" jazz-reggae sounds heard on several recent albums on the Concord and Island labels.

# SELECTED DISCOGRAPHY

| | |
|---|---|
| THIS IS MONTY ALEXANDER | VERVE VS 8790 (1969) |
| HERE COMES THE SUN | MPS 21.20913 (1971) |
| UNLIMITED LOVE | MPS 21.22781 (1974) |
| THE WAY IT IS | MPS 15484 (1976) |
| SOUL FUSION | PABLO 2310.804 (1977) |
| JAMENTO | PABLO 2310.826 (CD - OJC-904)(1976) |
| FACETS | CONCORD CJ 108 (CD - CCD 4108) (1979) |
| IVORY AND STEEL | CONCORD CJ 124 (CD - CCD 4124) (1980) |
| OVERSEAS SPECIAL/TO YOU EVERYWHERE | CONCORD CJ 253 (CD - CCD 4253) (1982) |
| THE DUKE ELLINGTON SONGBOOK | MPS 821 151 (CD) (1983) |
| FULL STEAM AHEAD | CONCORD CCD 4287 (CD) (1984) |
| FRIDAY NIGHT | LIMETREE 0022 (CD) (1985) |
| SATURDAY NIGHT | LIMETREE 0024 (CD) (1985) |
| THE RIVER | CONCORD CCD 4422 (CD) (1985) |
| JAMBOREE (W/IVORY AND STEEL) | CONCORD CCD 4359 (CD) (1988) |
| CARIBBEAN CIRCLE | CHESKY JD 80 (CD) (1992) |
| STEAMIN' | CONCORD CCD 4636 (CD) (1994) |
| AT MAYBECK (RECITAL HALL SERIES - VOLUME 40) | CONCORD CCD 4658 (CD) (1995) |
| YARD MOVEMENT | ISLAND JAMAICA JAZZ (POLYGRAM 524 232 (CD) (1995) |
| TO THE ENDS OF THE EARTH (W/IVORY AND STEEL) | CONCORD PICANTE CCD 4721 (CD) (1996) |
| ECHOES OF JILLY'S | CONCORD PICANTE CCD 4769 (CD) (1997) |

**TRIO WITH RAY BROWN AND HERB ELLIS:**

| | |
|---|---|
| TRIO | CONCORD CJ 136 (CD - CCD 4136) (1980) |
| TRIPLE THREAT | CONCORD CJ 193 (CD - CCD 4193) (1982) |
| TRIPLE THREAT II | CONCORD CCD 4338 (CD) (1987) |
| TRIPLE THREAT III | CONCORD CCD 4394 (CD) (1987) |

Monty has been a sideman on the recordings of Kai Winding, Milt Jackson, Dizzy Gillespie, Ernestine Anderson, Marshall Royal, Johnny Griffin, Shelly Manne, Jimmy Smith, Barney Kessel, and Howard Alden.

# THE MONTY ALEXANDER
## COLLECTION
# CONTENTS

# JAMENTO

Written by MONTY ALEXANDER

**Latin Two Step (straight eighths)**

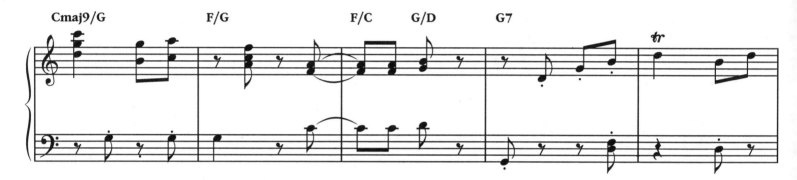

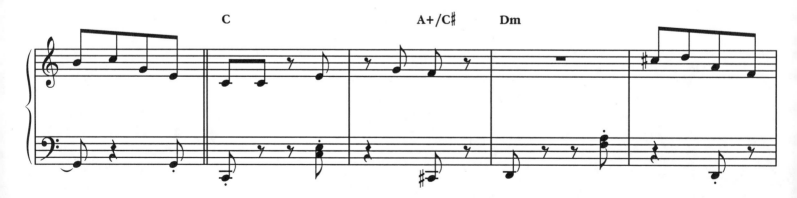

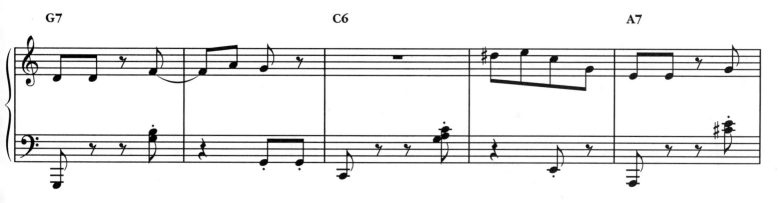

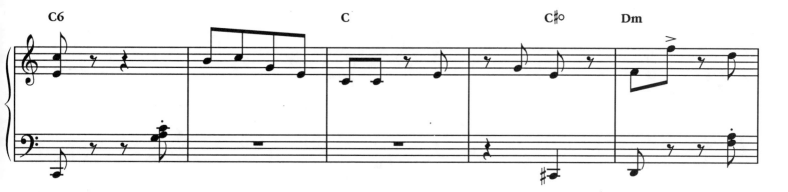

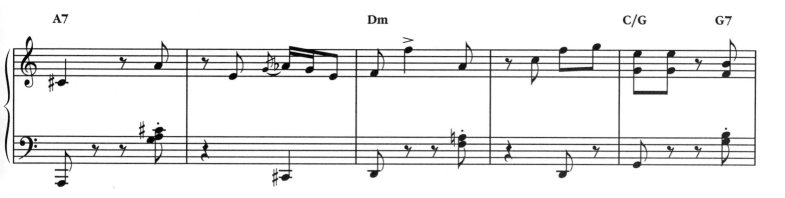

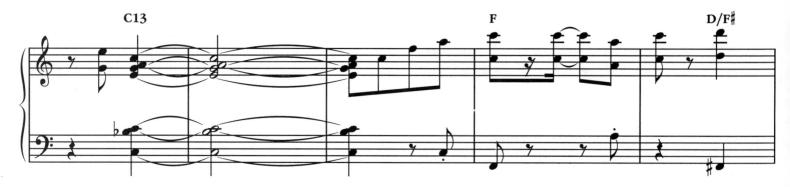

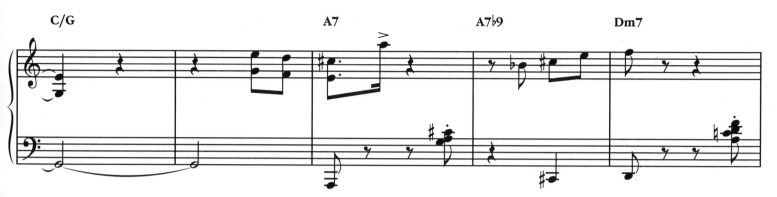

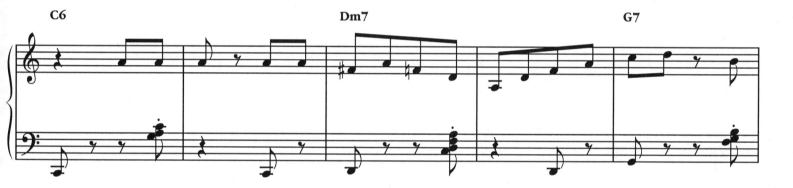

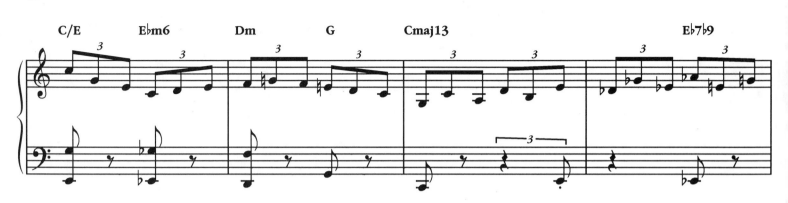

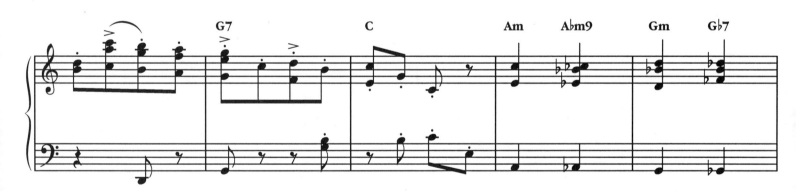

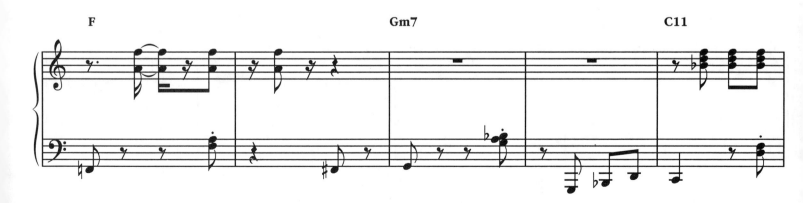

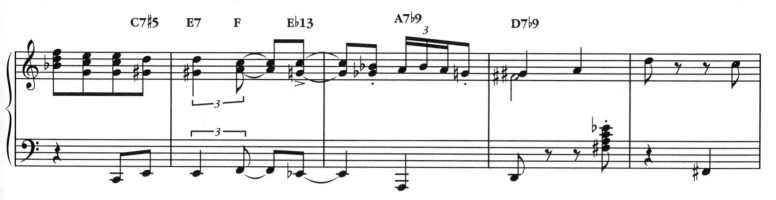

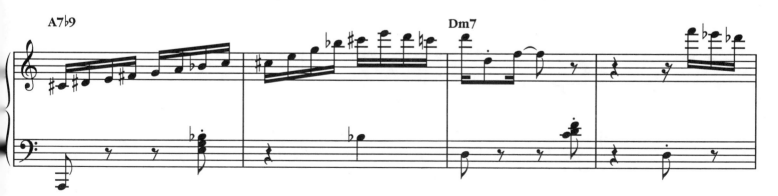

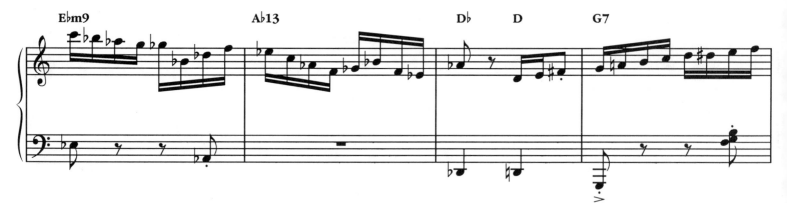

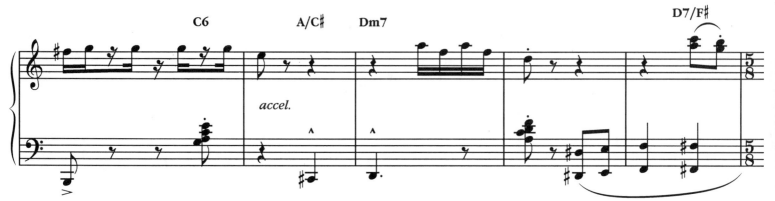

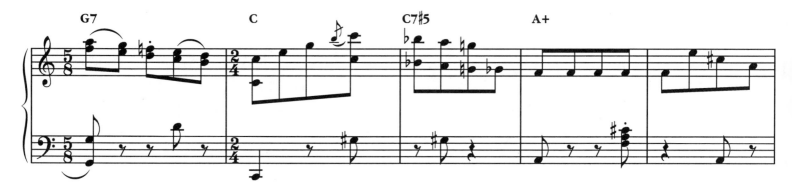

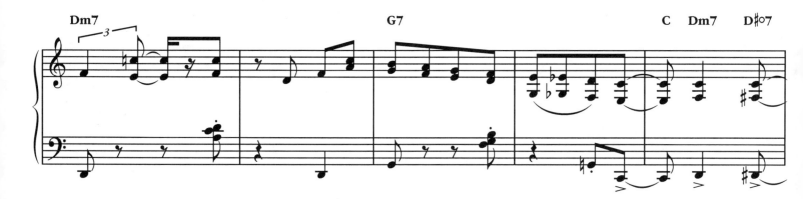

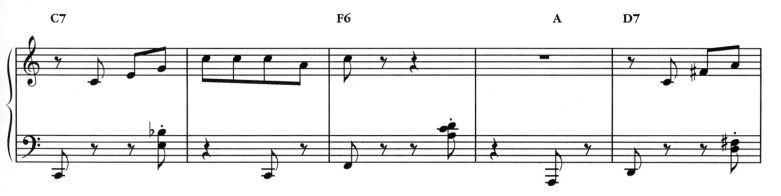

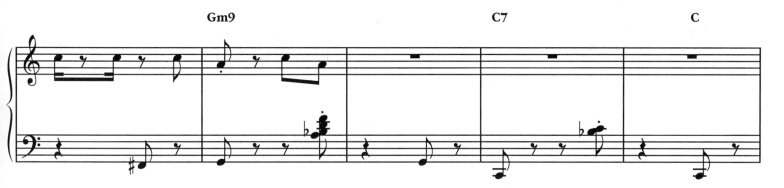

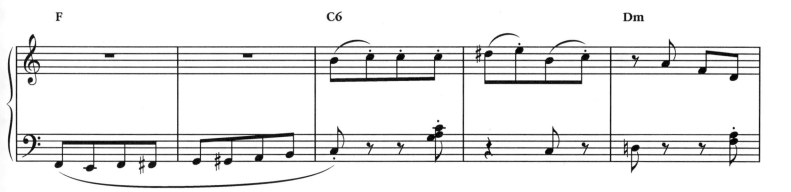

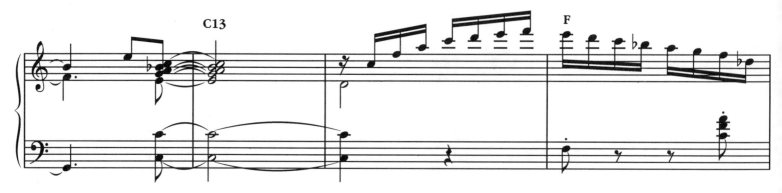

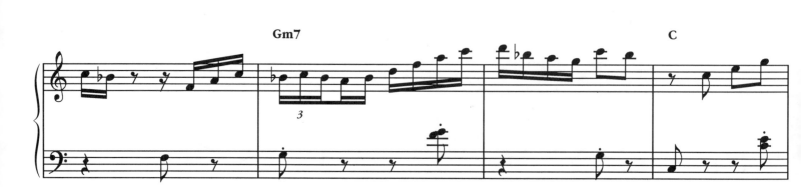

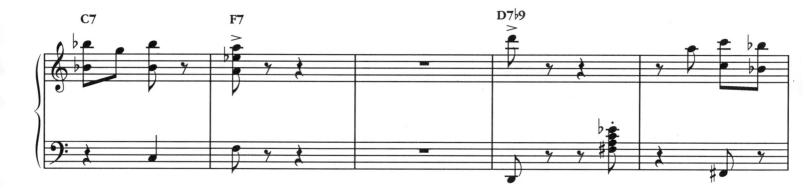

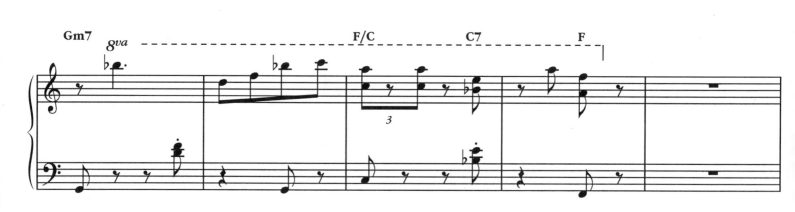

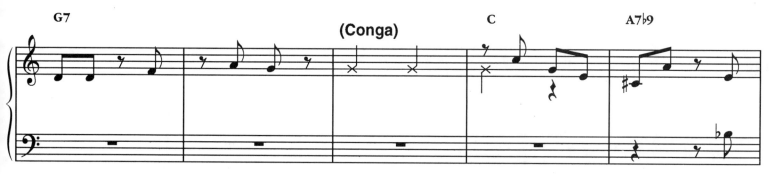

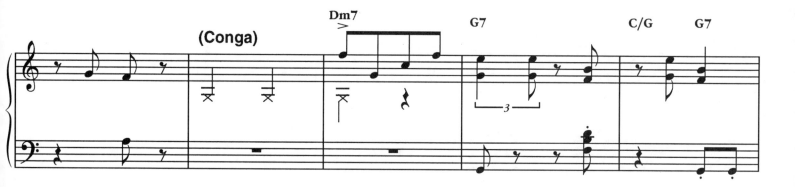

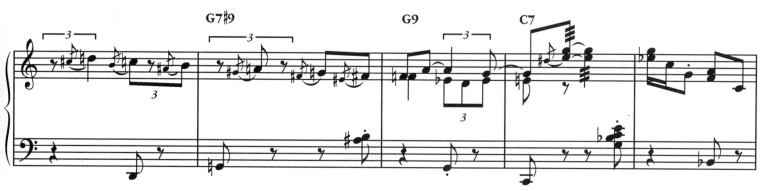

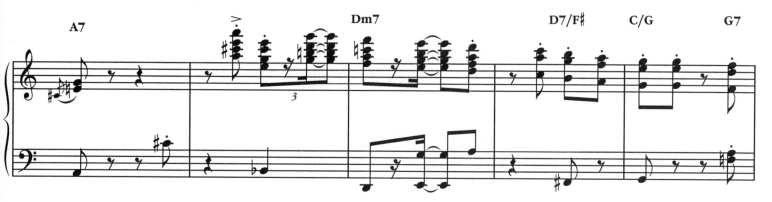

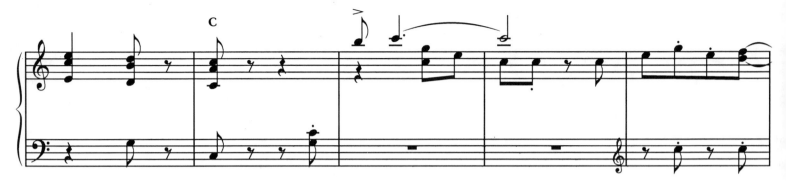

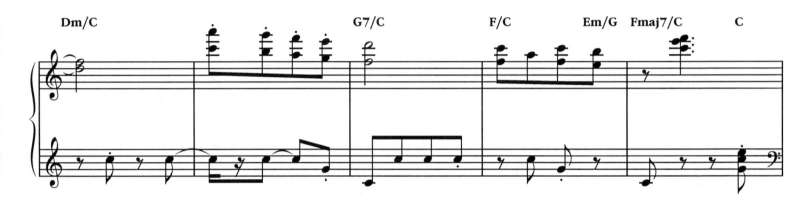

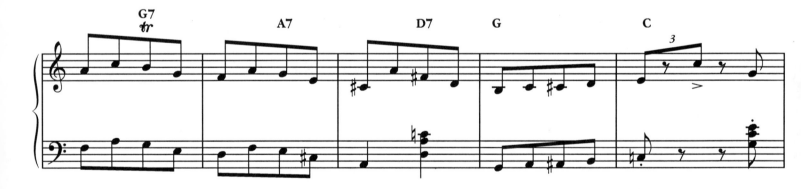

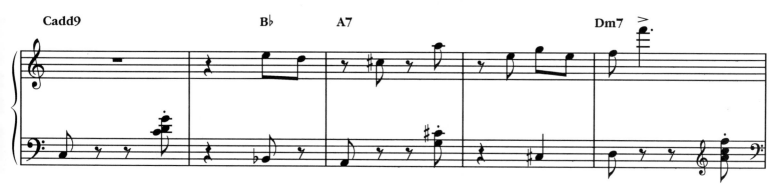

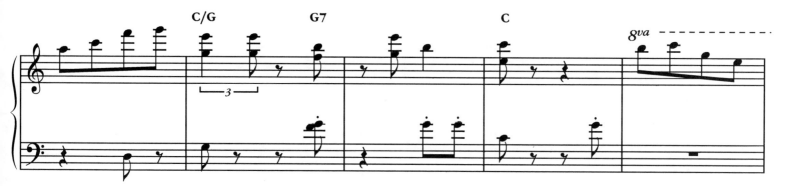

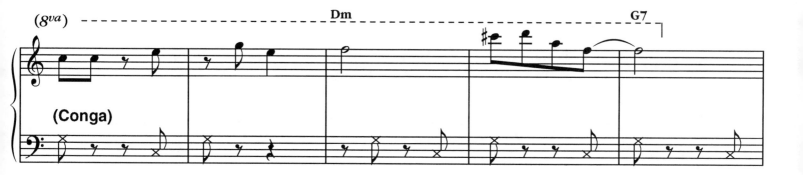

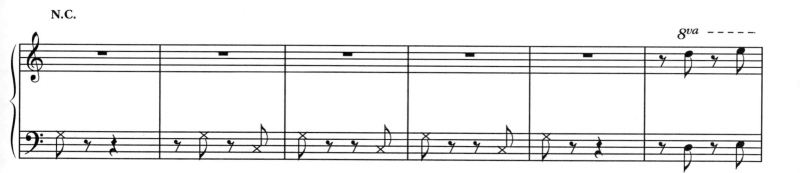

# HAPPY LYPSO

**Written by MONTY ALEXANDER**

20

## Steel Drum Solo

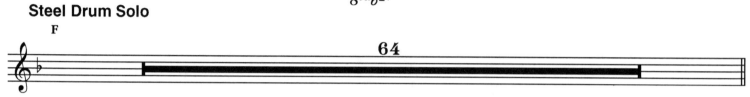

**64**

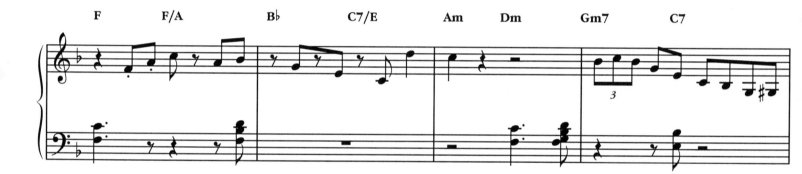

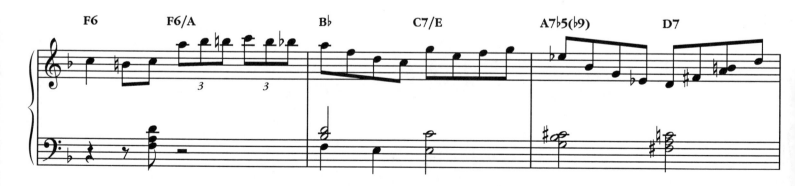

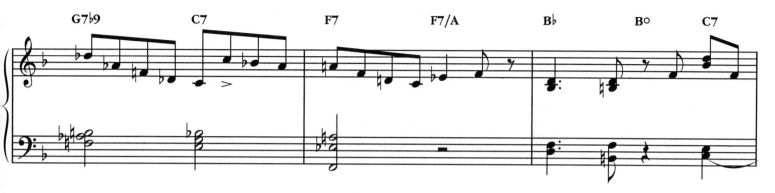

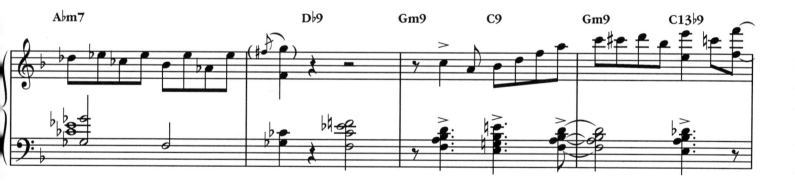

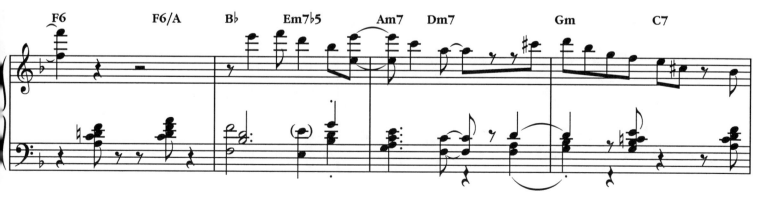

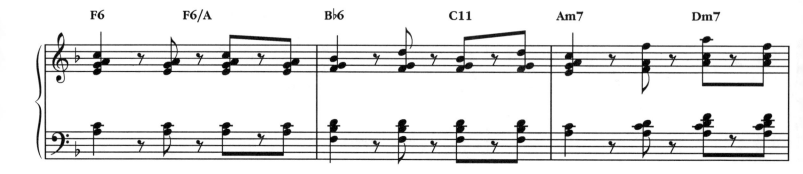

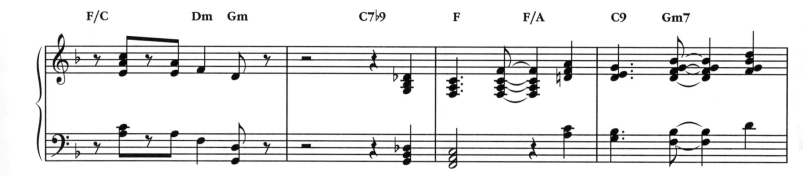

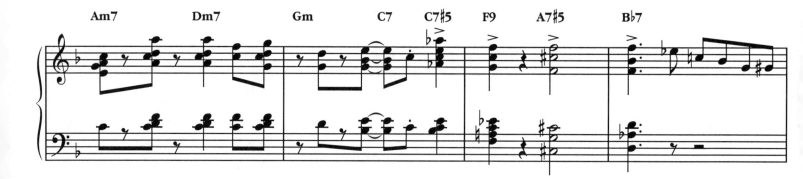

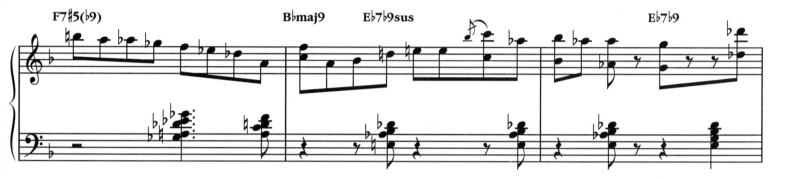

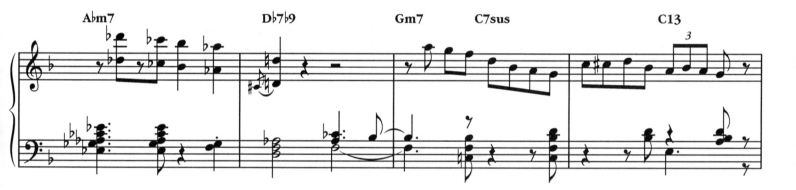

24

**Steel Drum**

Piano cont. ad lib.

**Steel Drum Solo**

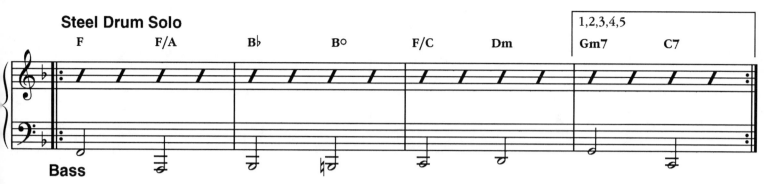

**Bass**

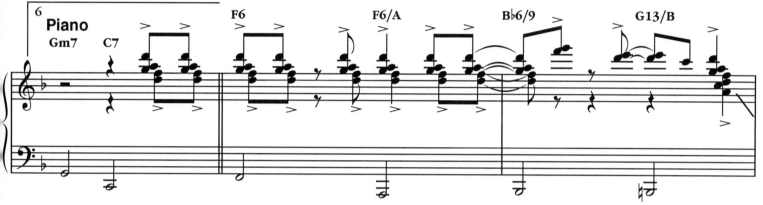

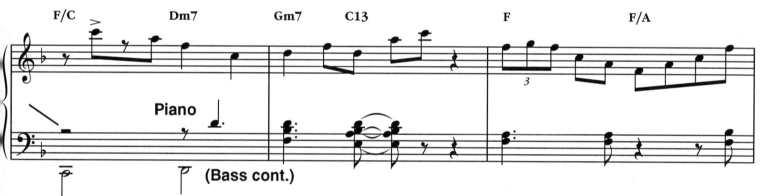

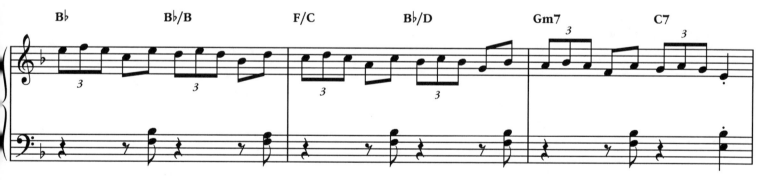

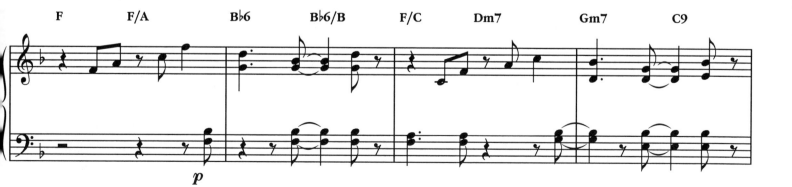

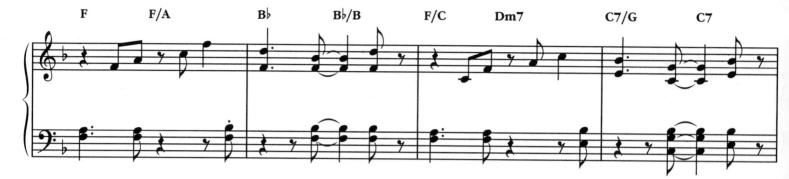

**Steel Drum**

Piano cont. ad lib.

**(Ride out piano solo)**

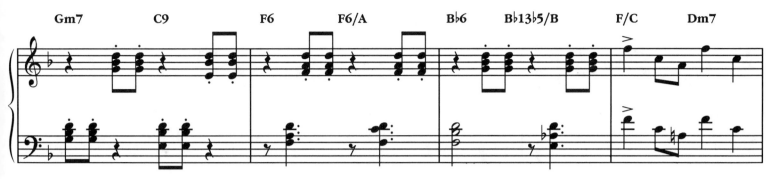

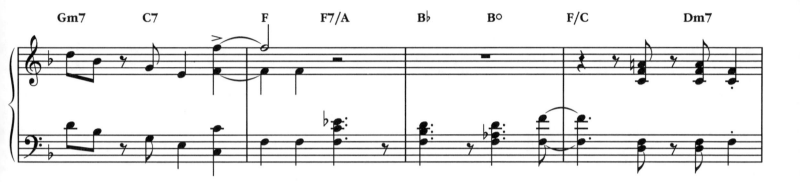

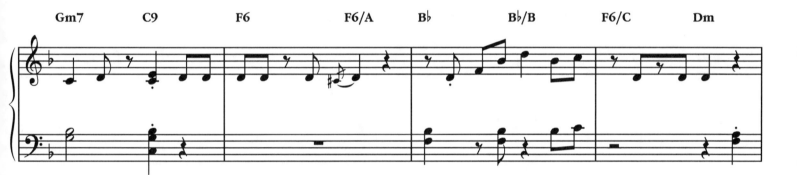

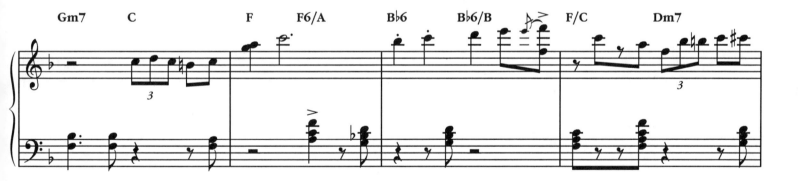

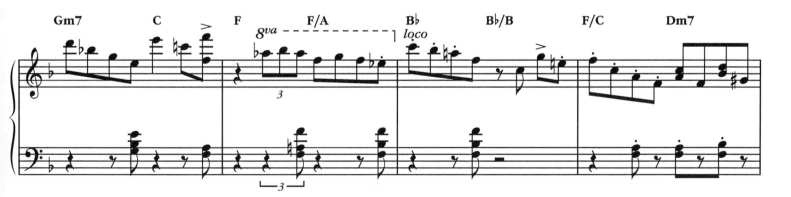

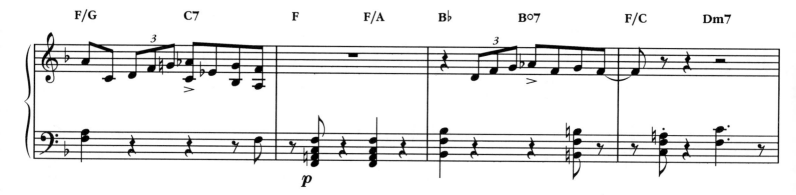

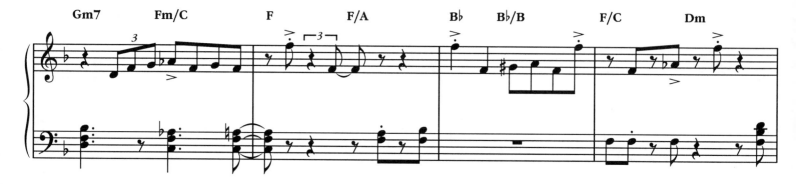

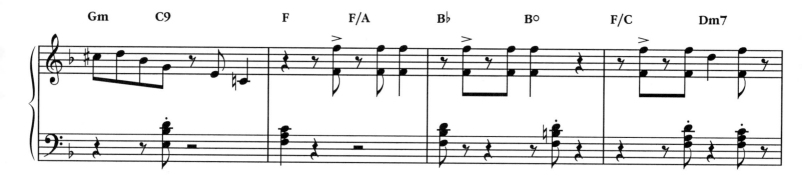

# REGGAE-LATER

Written by MONTY ALEXANDER

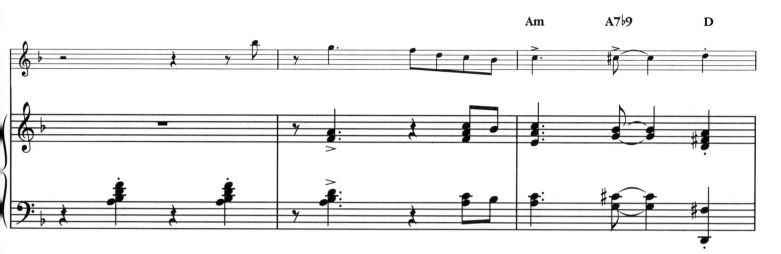

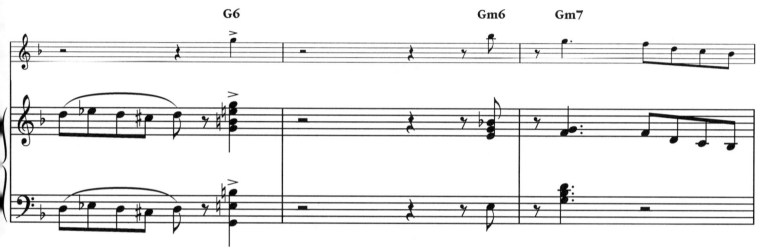

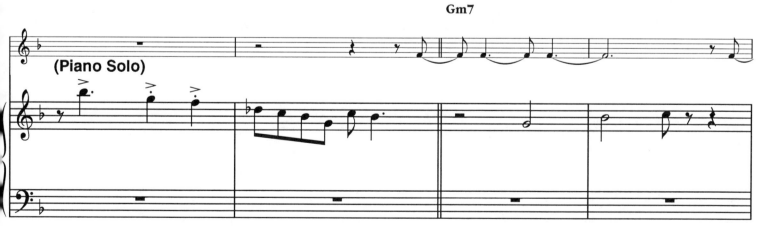

(Piano Solo)

**(Steel drums cont. comp.)**

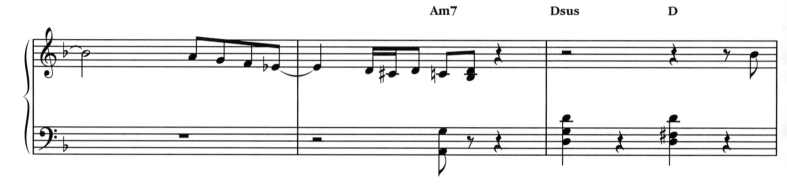

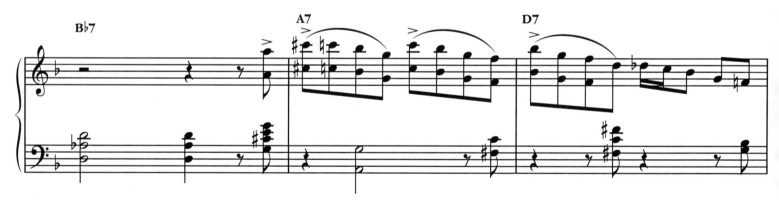

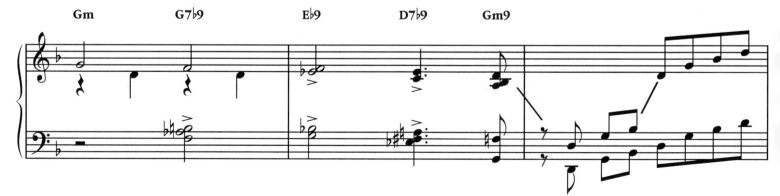

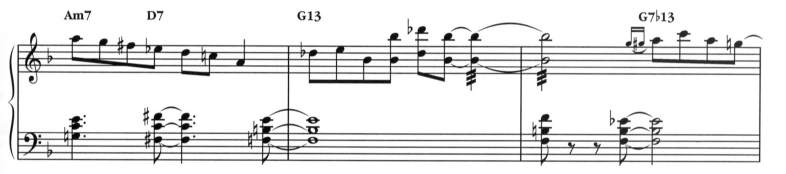

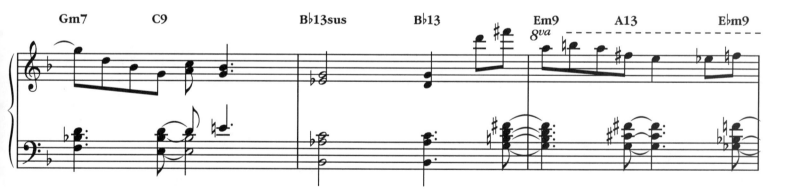

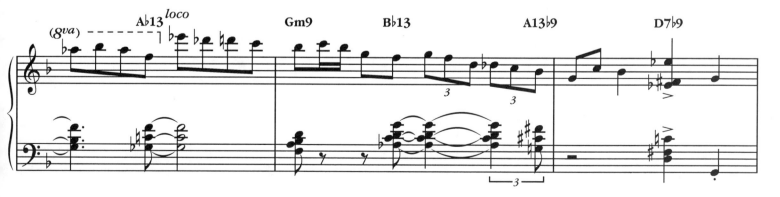

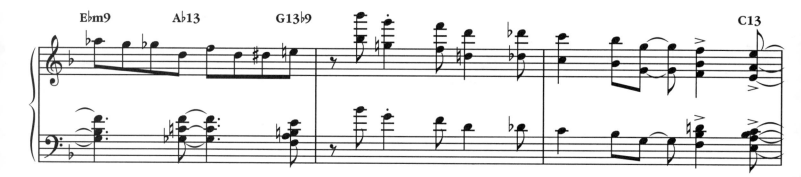

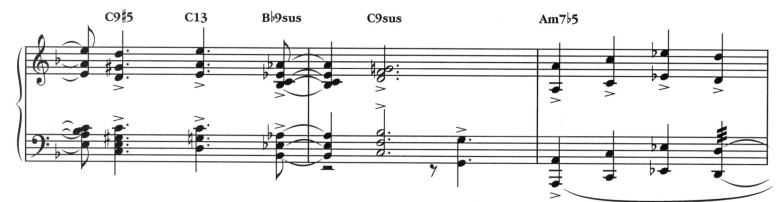

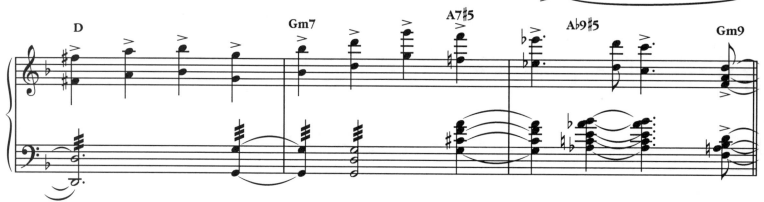

**Steel Drum Solos**

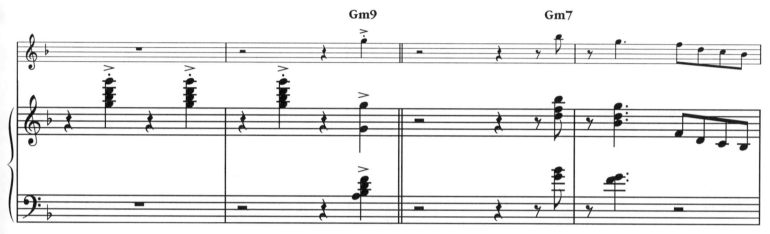

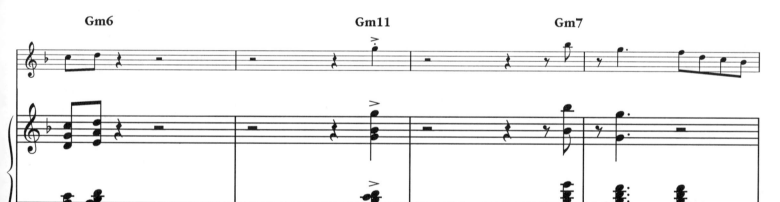

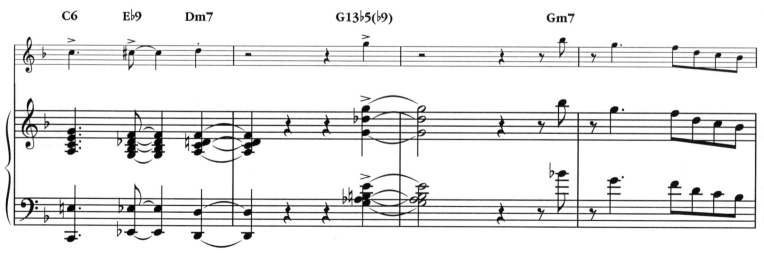

page

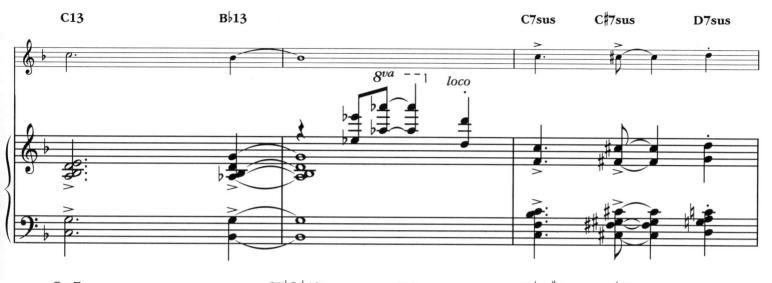

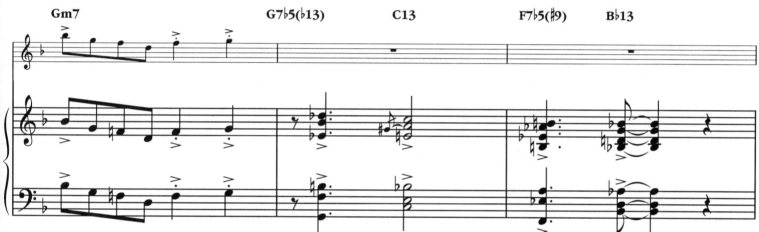

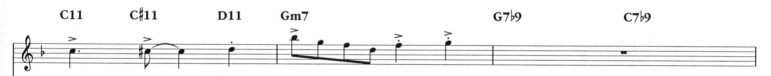

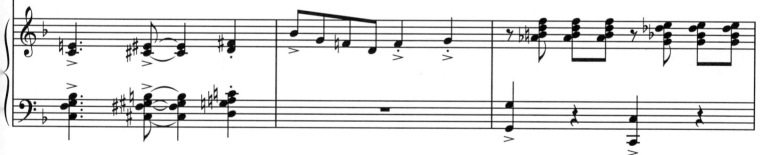

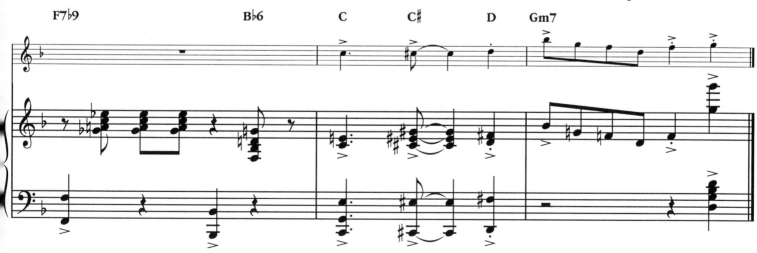

# LOOK UP

Written by MONTY ALEXANDER

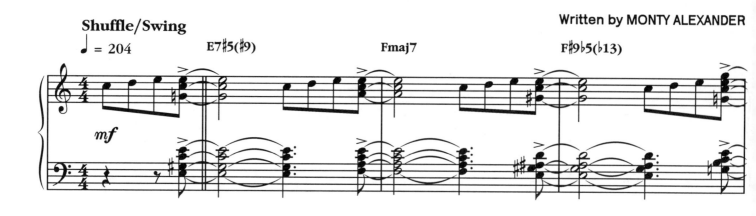

**Steel Drums**
**2nd doubled 8vb**

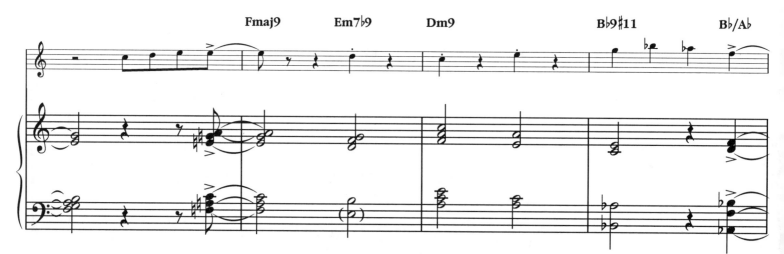

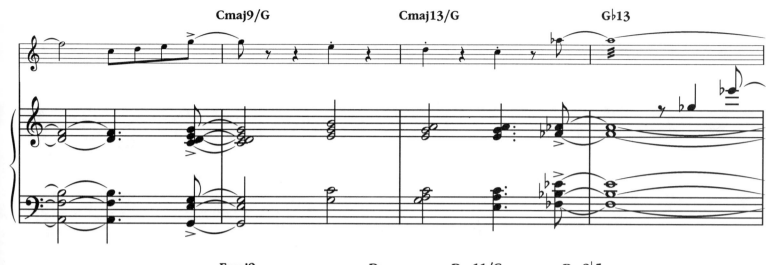

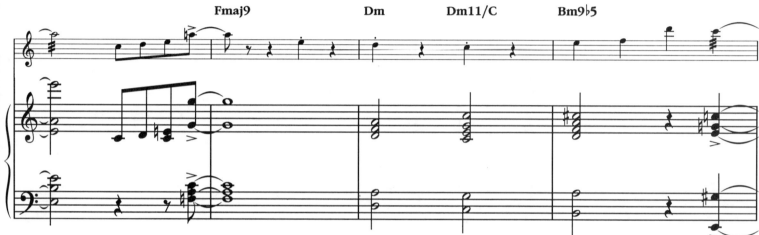

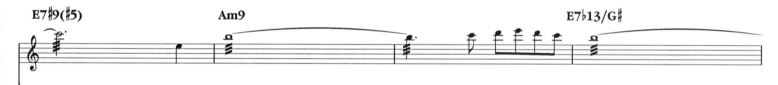

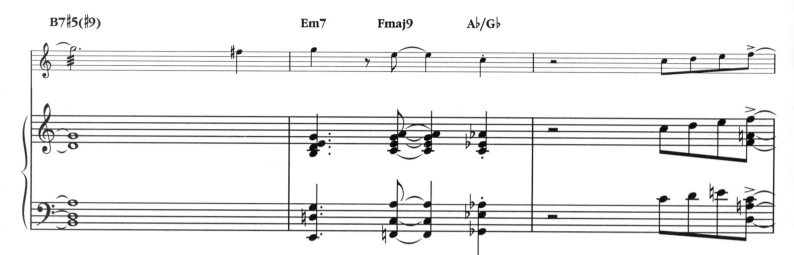

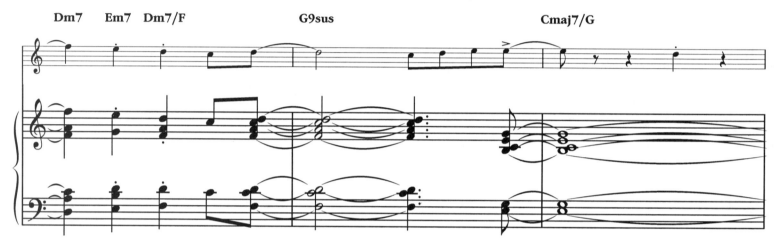

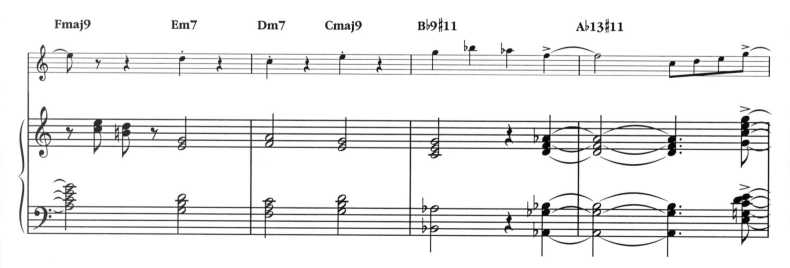

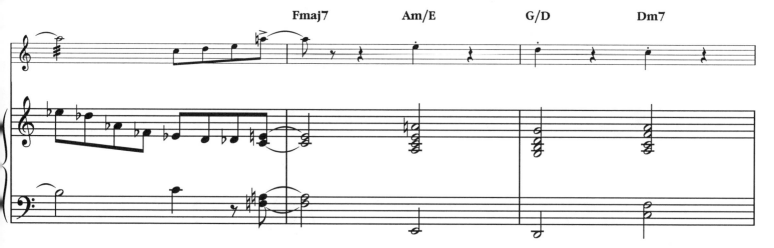

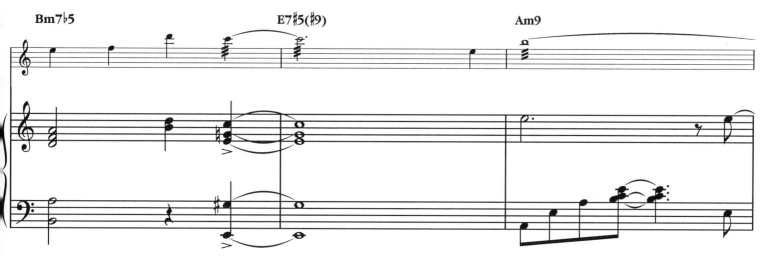

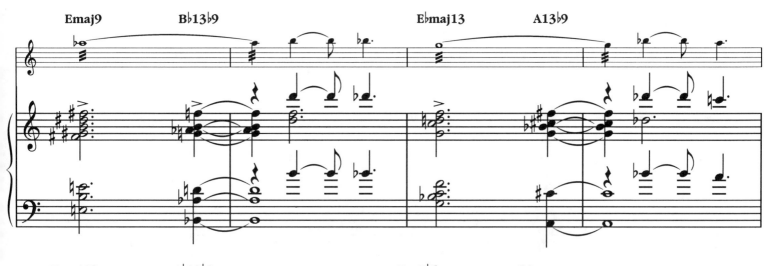

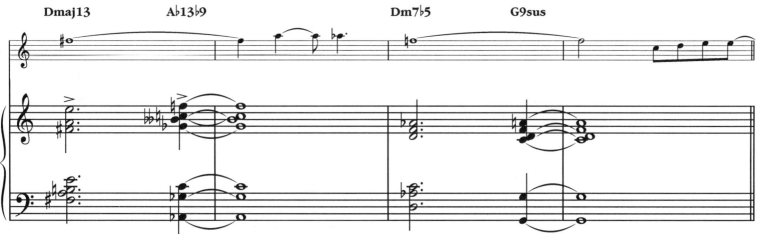

**Steel Drums**

(Piano cont. ad-lib)

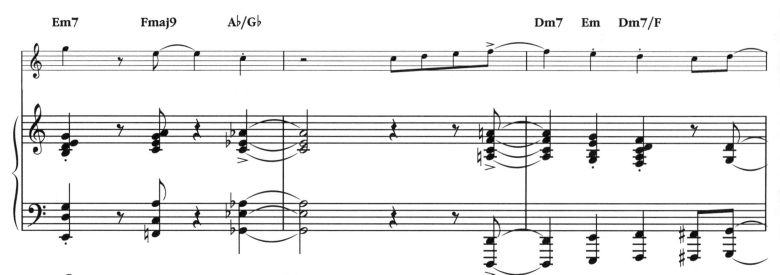

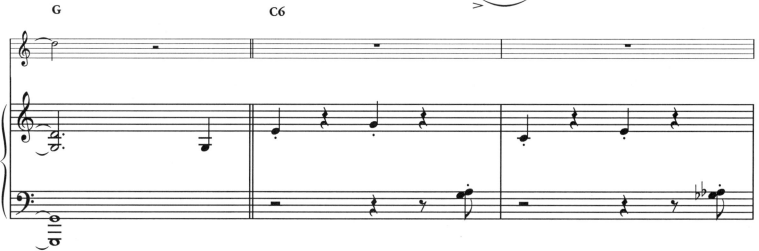

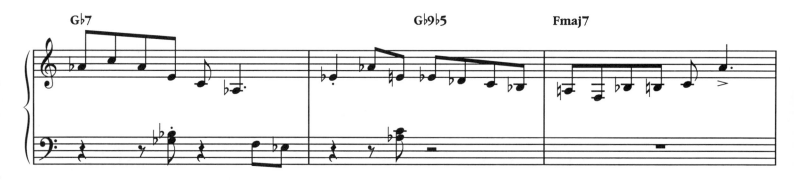

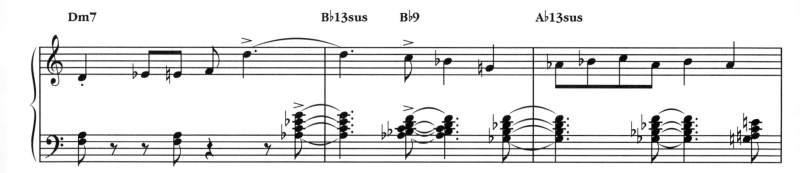

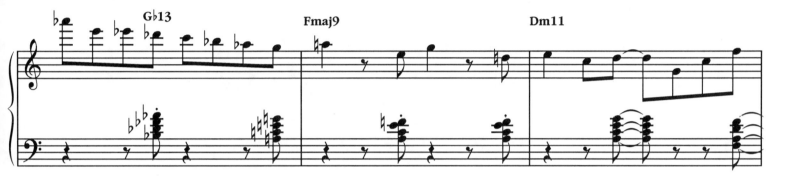

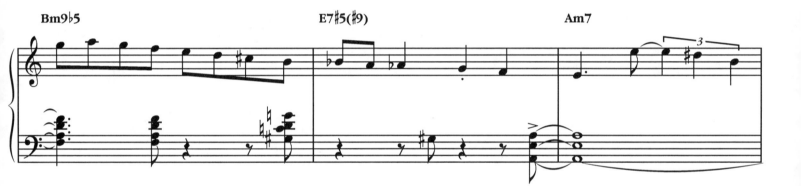

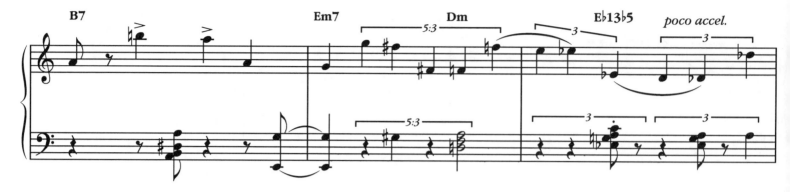

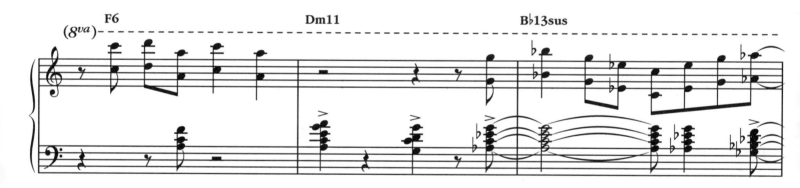

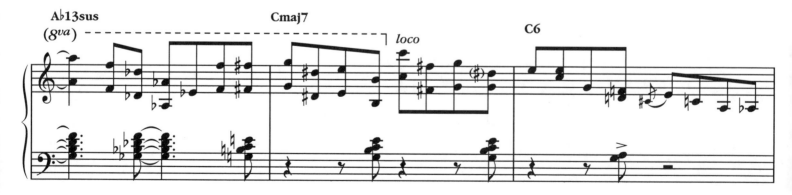

**Steel Drums**

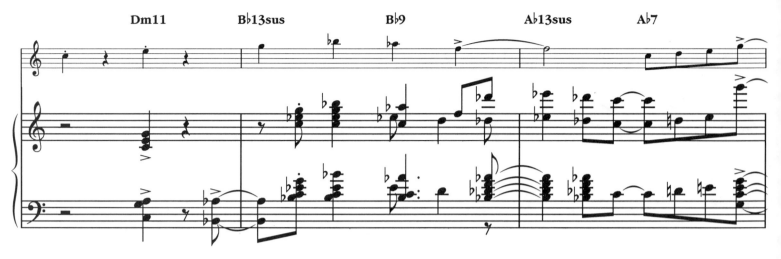

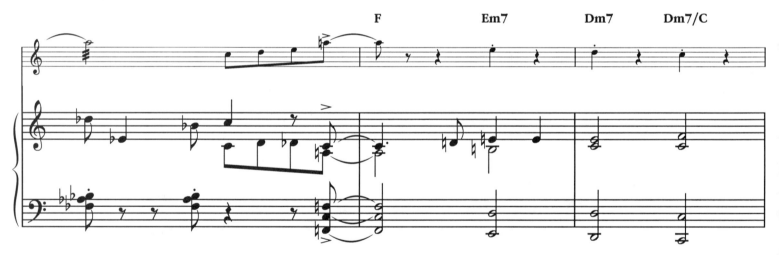

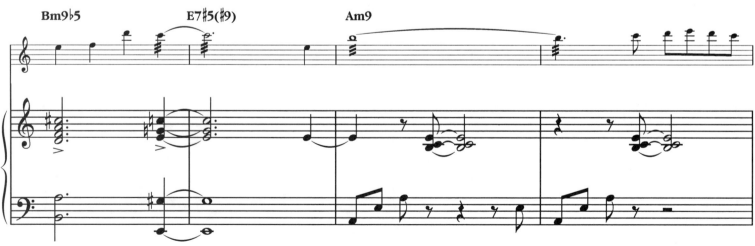

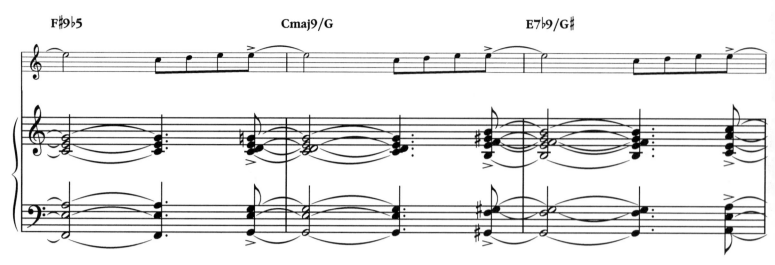

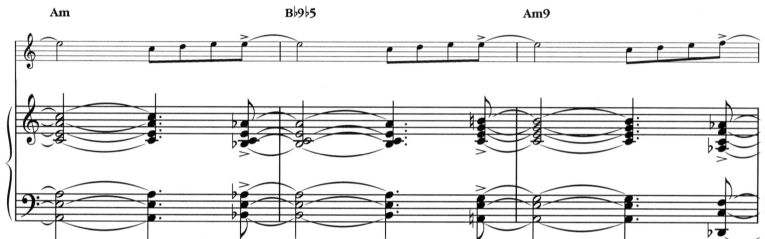

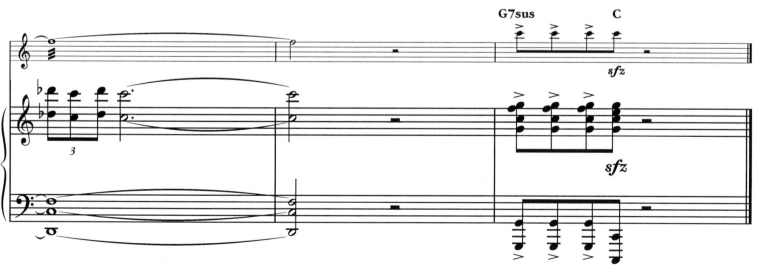

# THE RIVER

**Written by MONTY ALEXANDER**

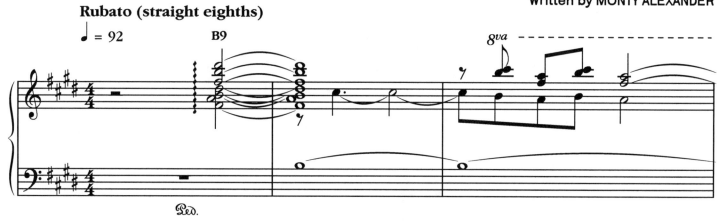

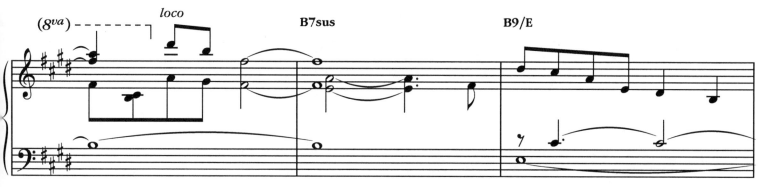

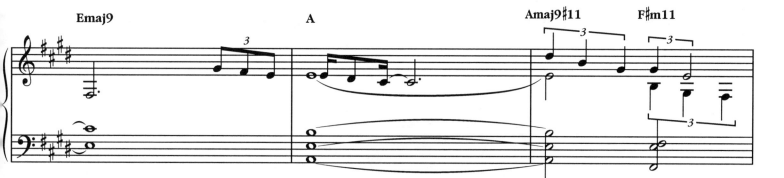

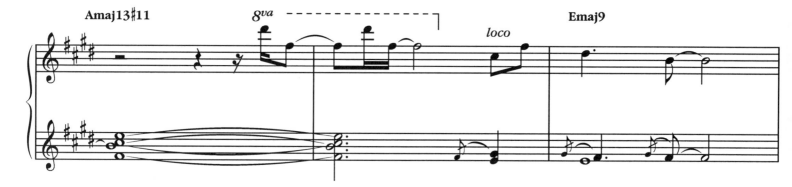

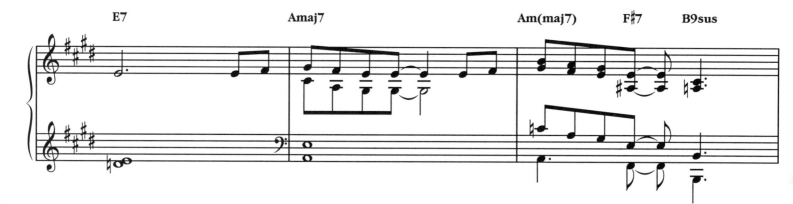

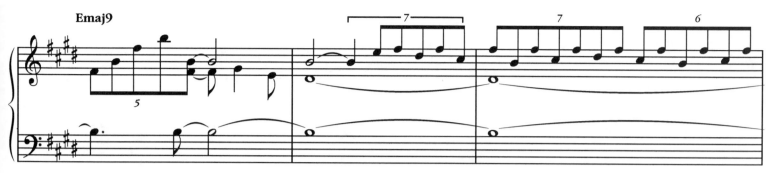

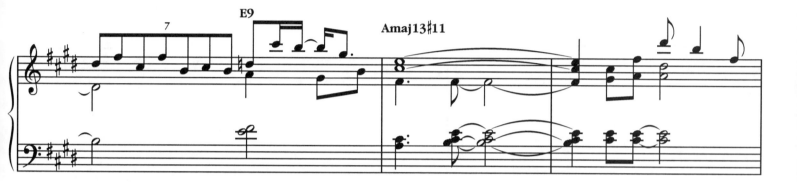

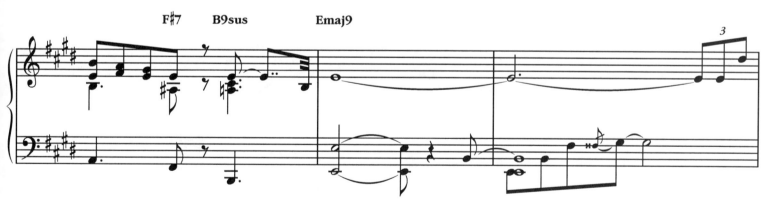

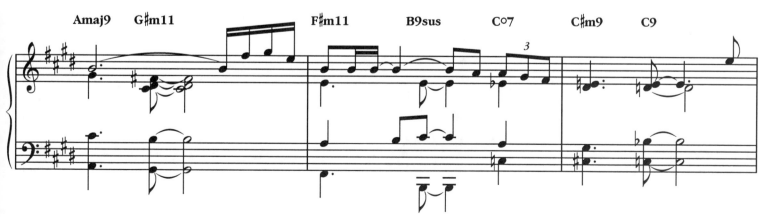

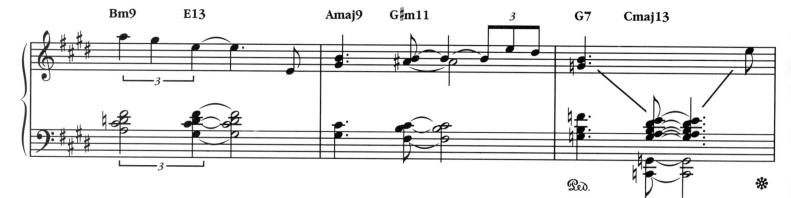

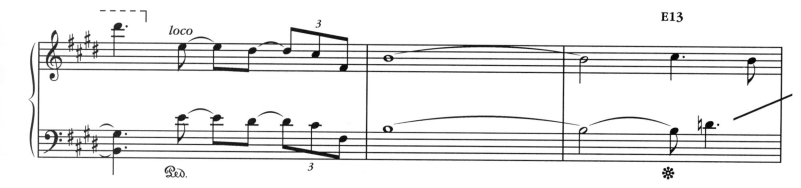

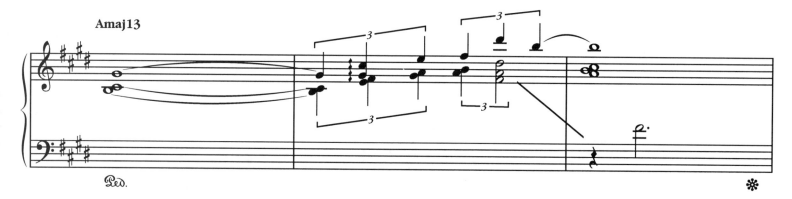

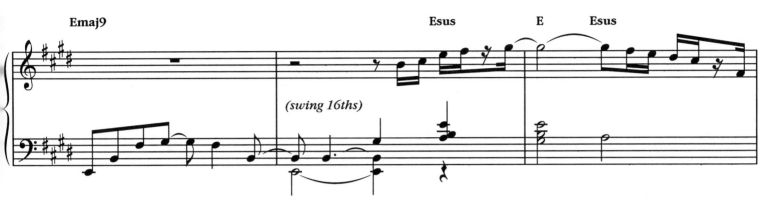

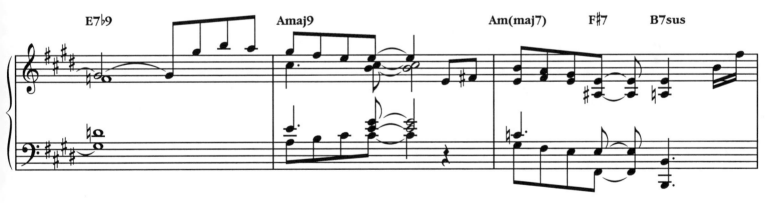

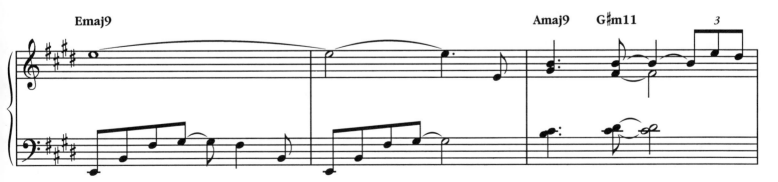

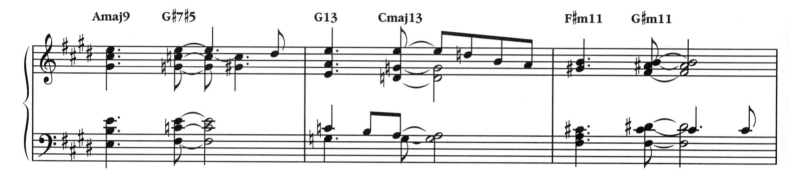

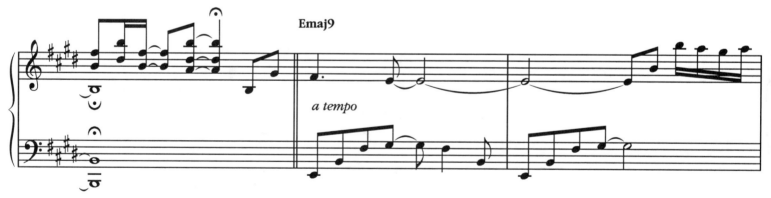

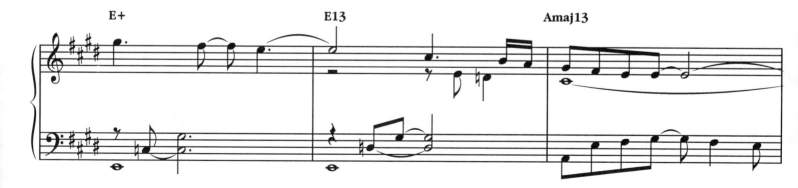

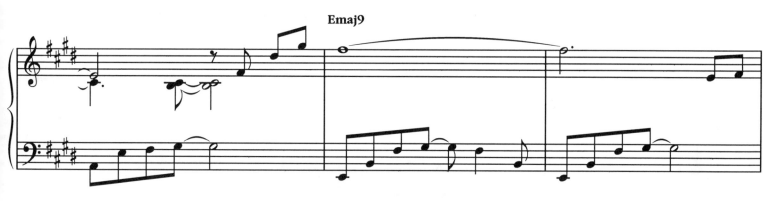

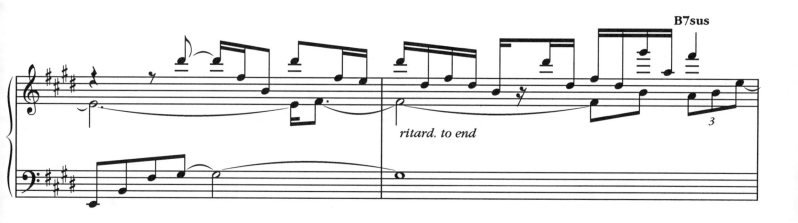

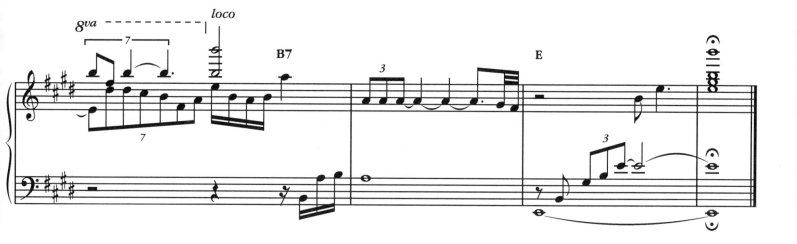

# THINK TWICE

Written by MONTY ALEXANDER

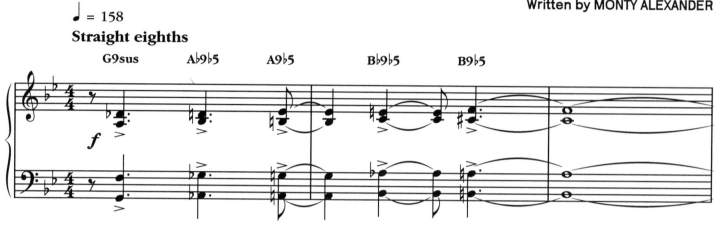

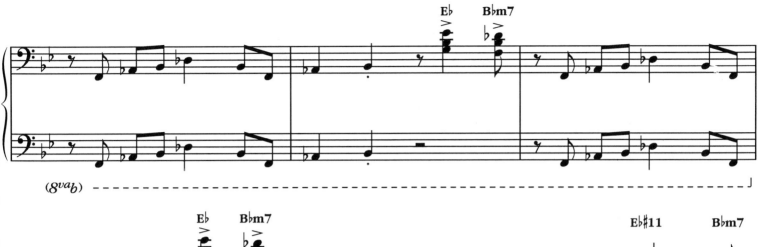

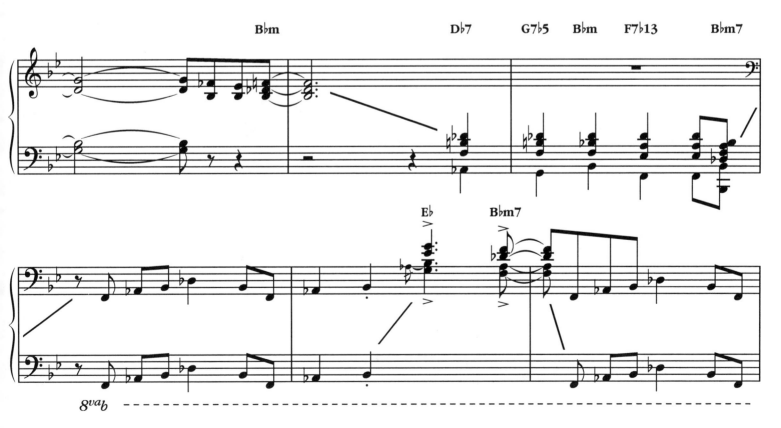

**Bass**

**Piano**

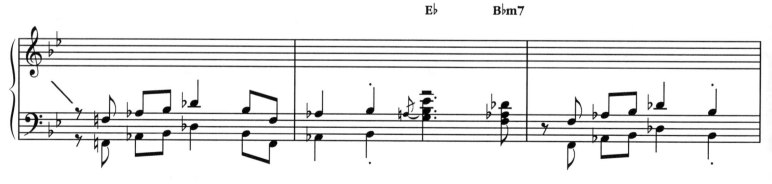

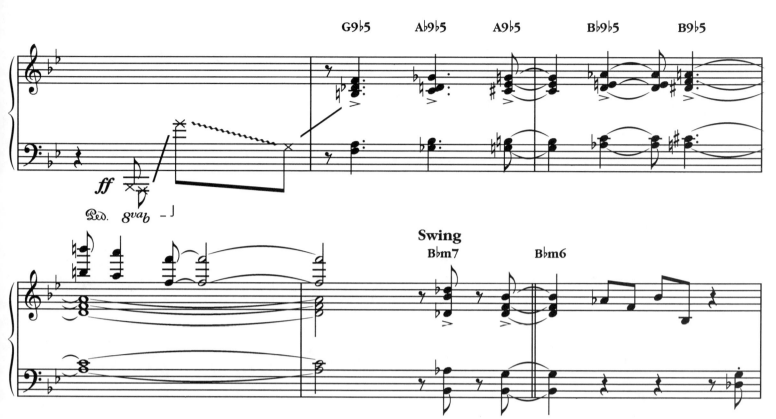

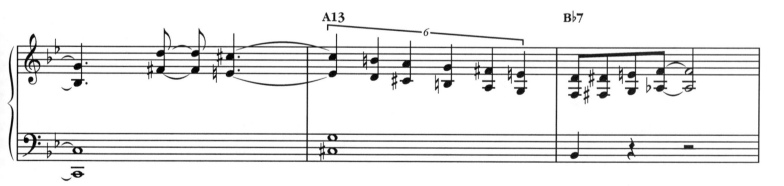

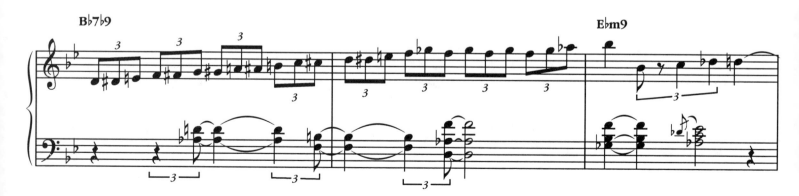

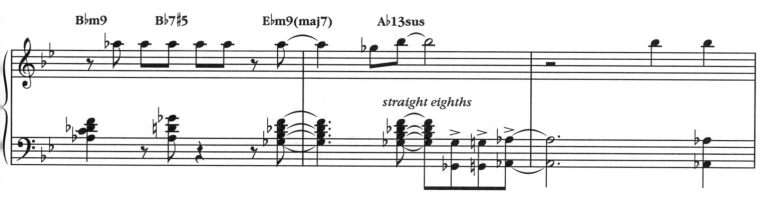

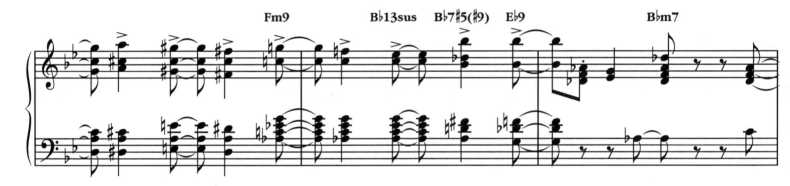

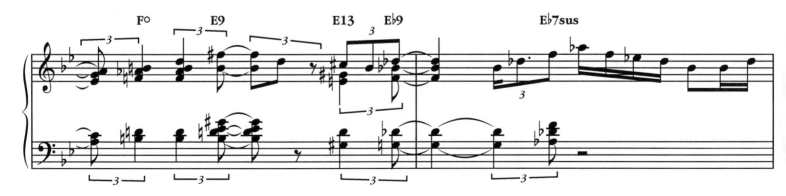

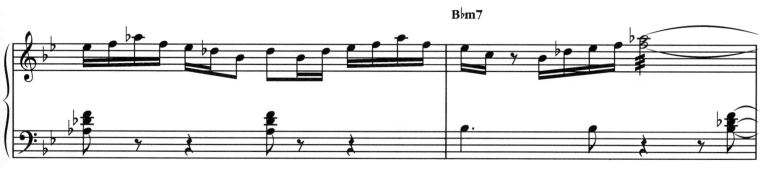

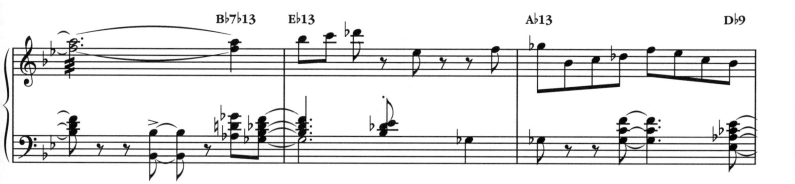

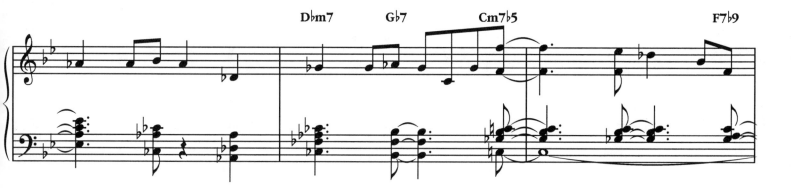

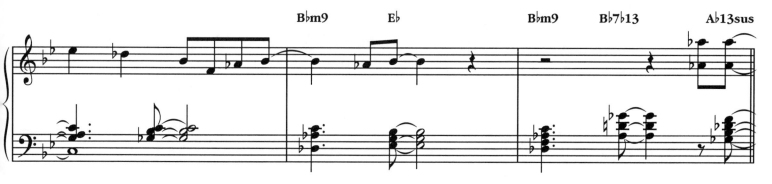

(Steel drum enters)

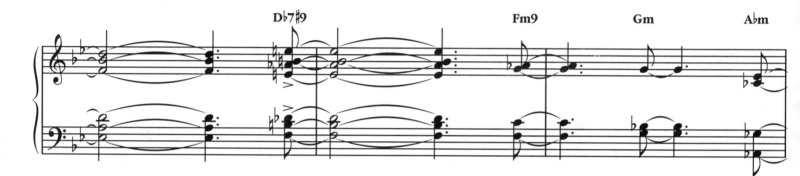

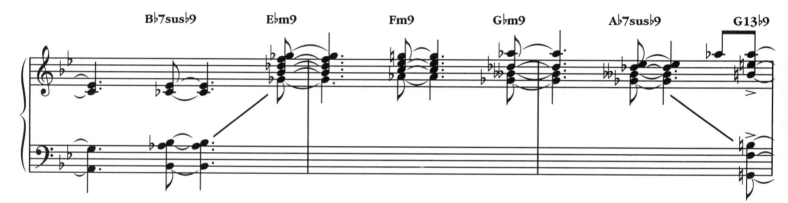

Steel drum cont. with melody 8va
as piano comps

*straight eighths*

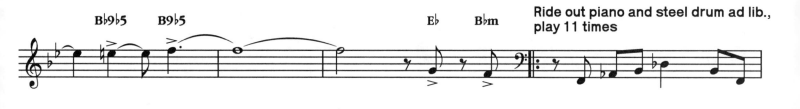

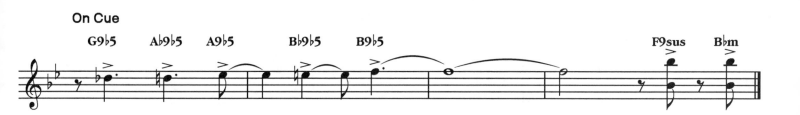

# YOU CAN SEE

Written by MONTY ALEXANDER

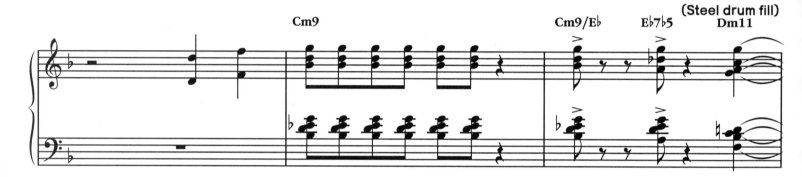

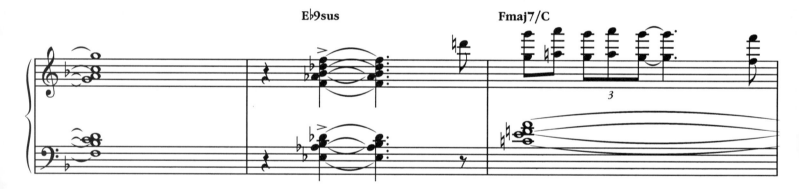

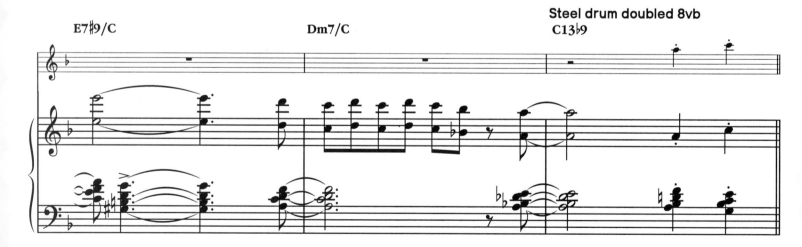

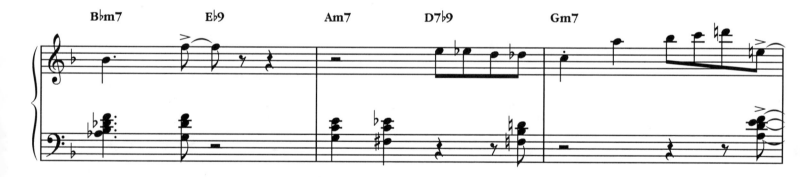

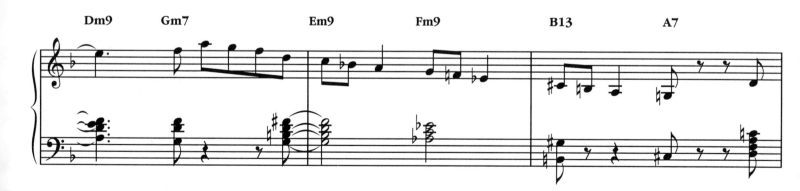

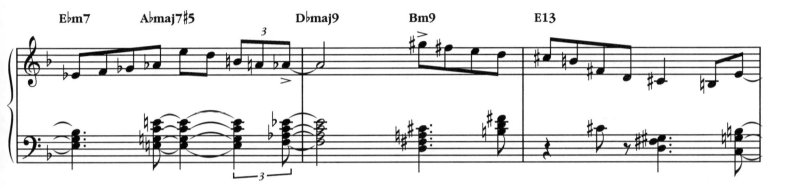

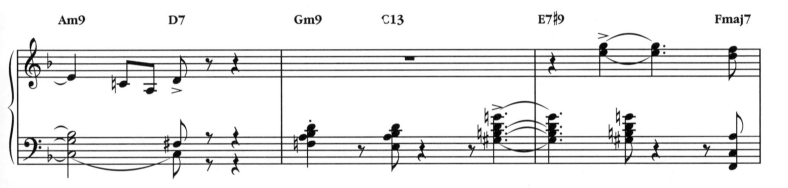

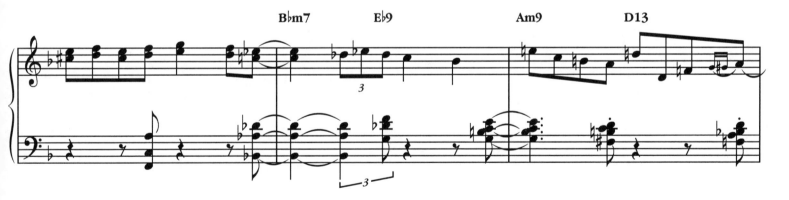

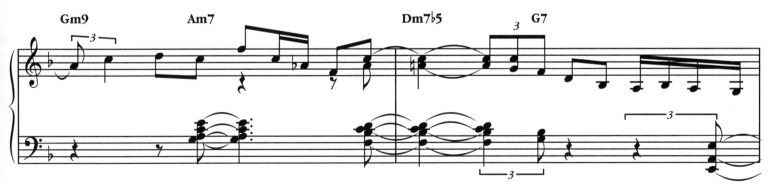

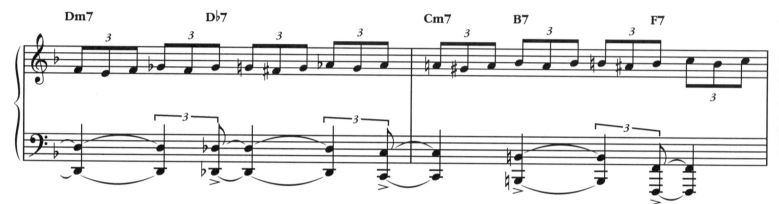

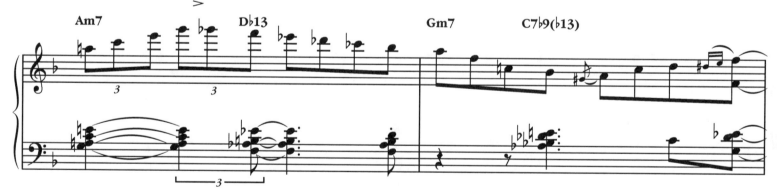

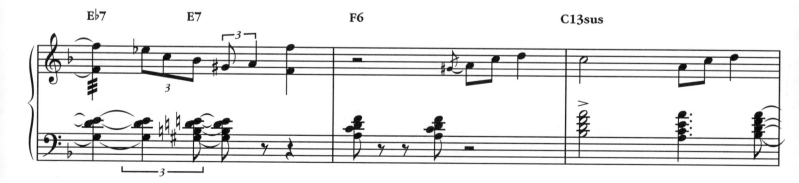

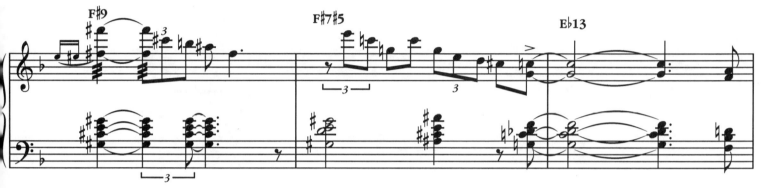

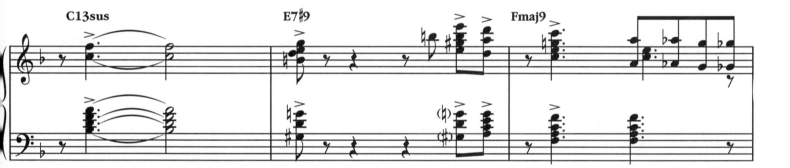

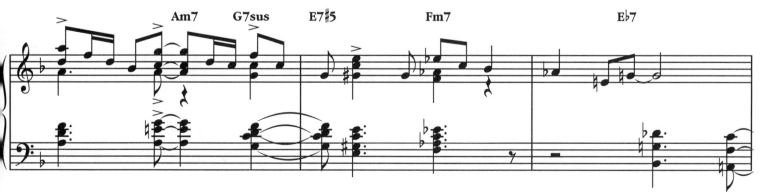

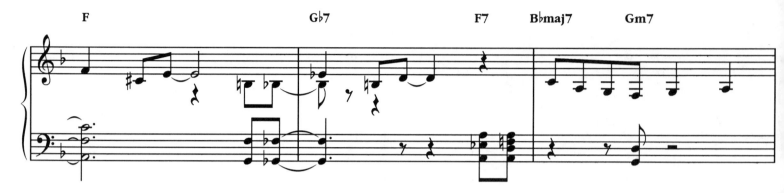

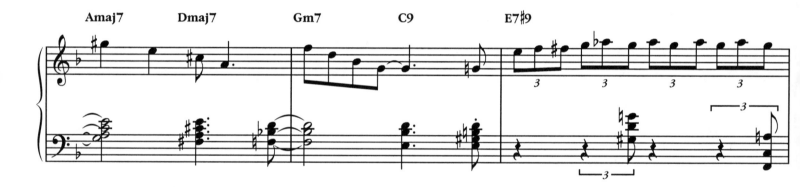

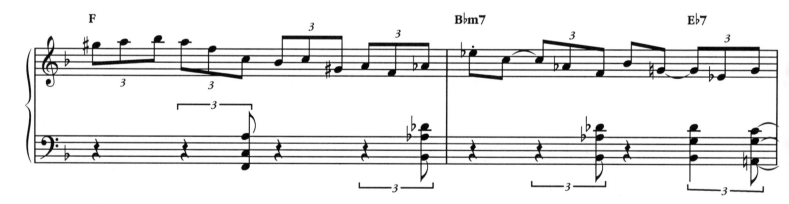

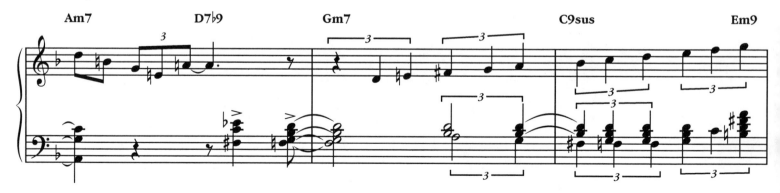

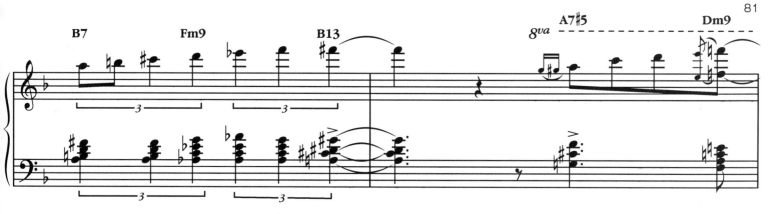

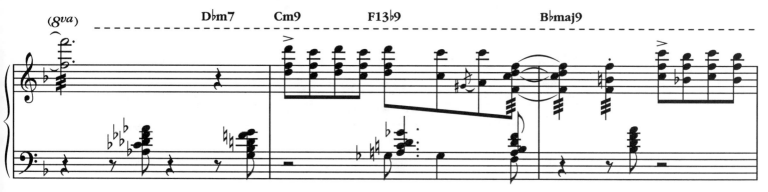

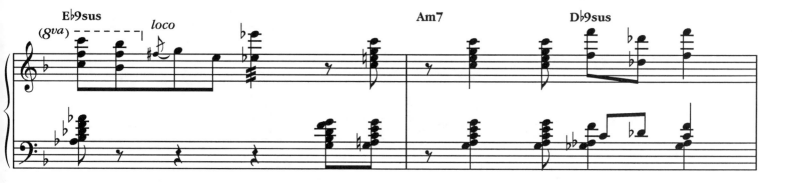

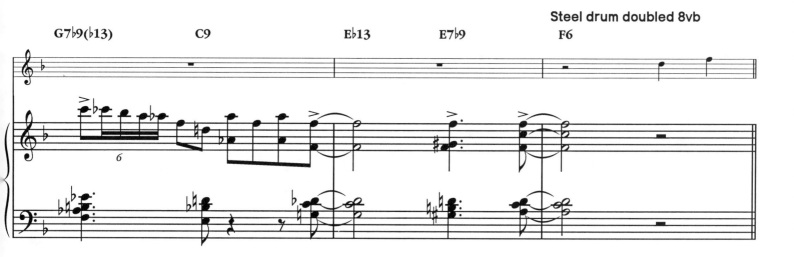

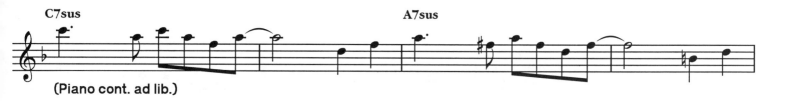

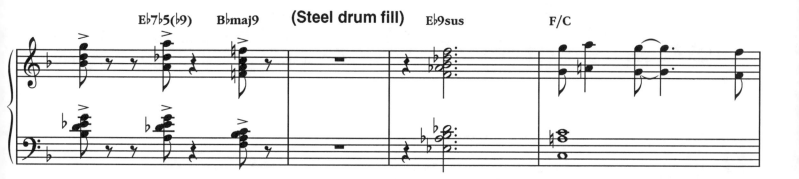

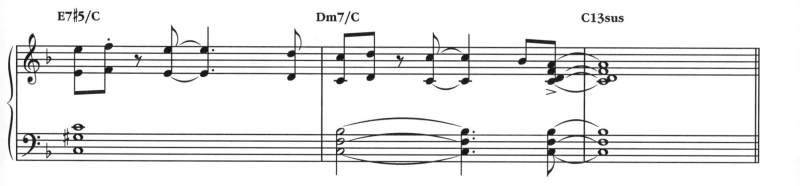

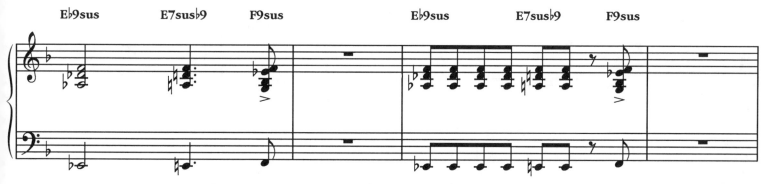

# RENEWAL

Written by MONTY ALEXANDER

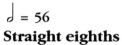

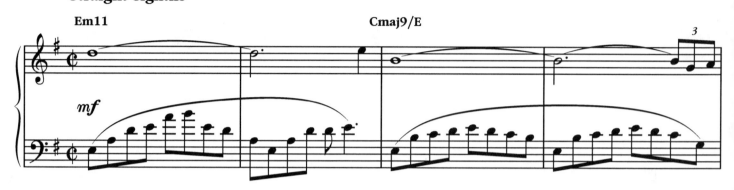

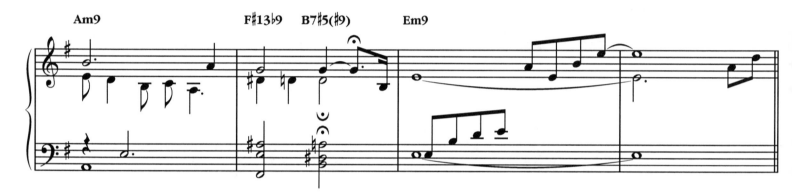

**Quasi rubato**

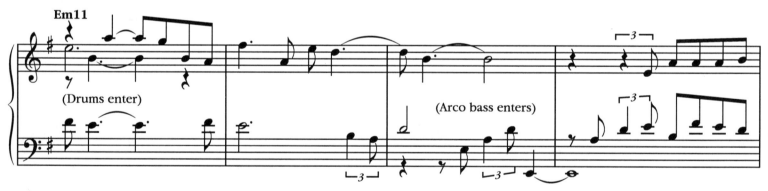

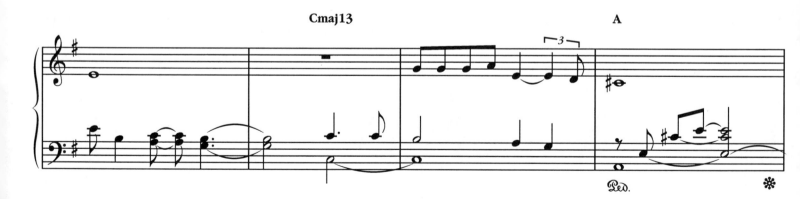

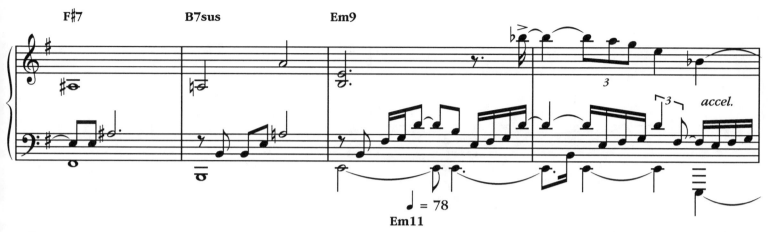

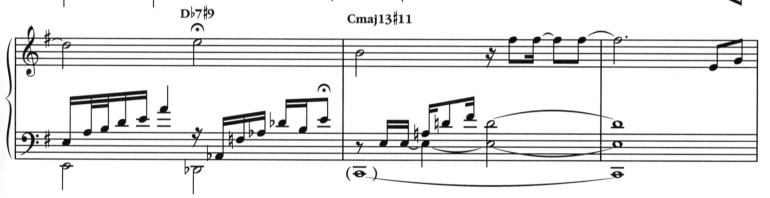

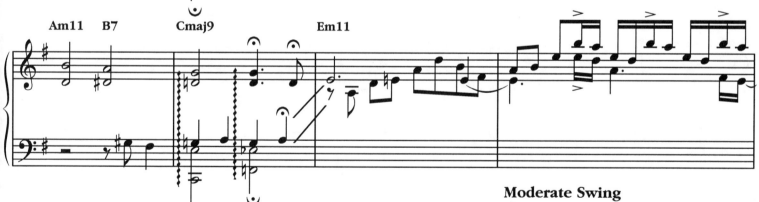

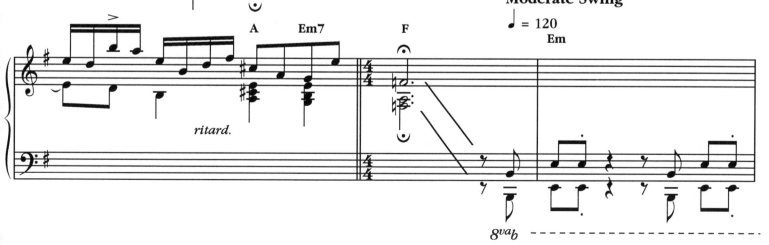

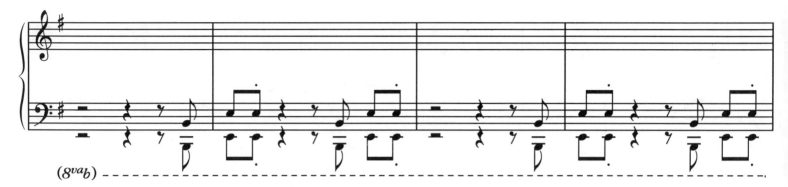

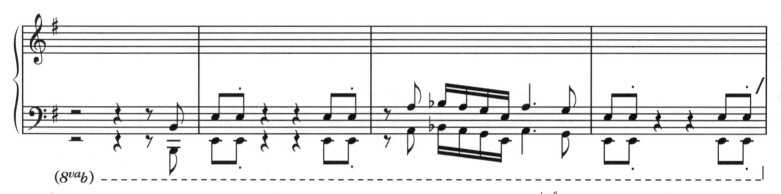

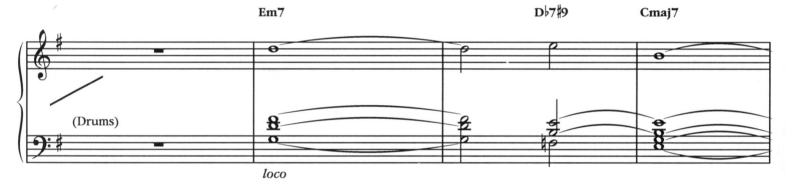

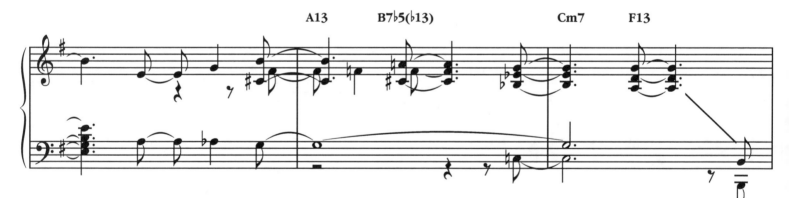

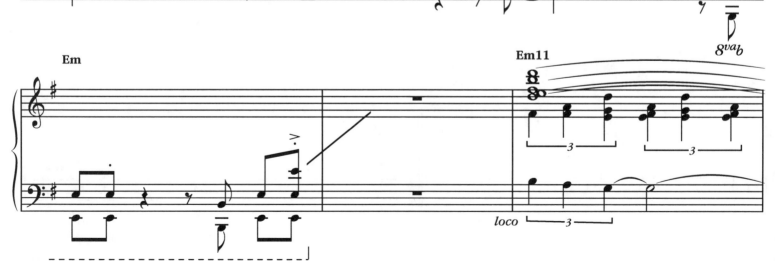

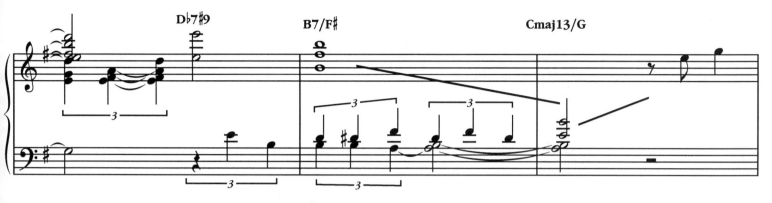

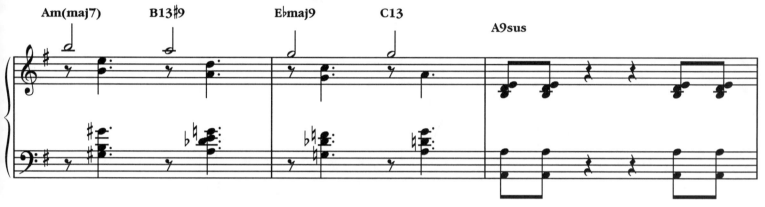

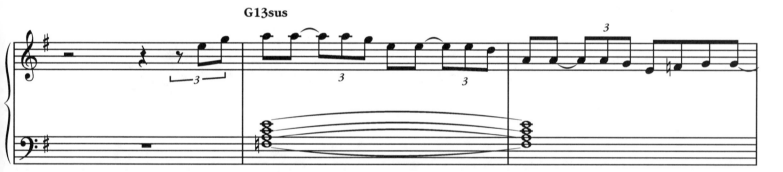

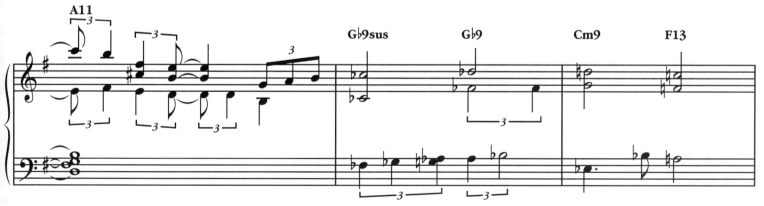

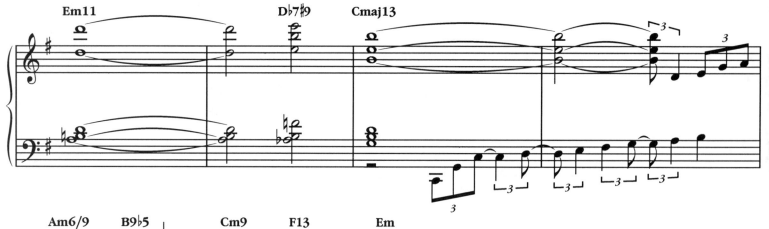

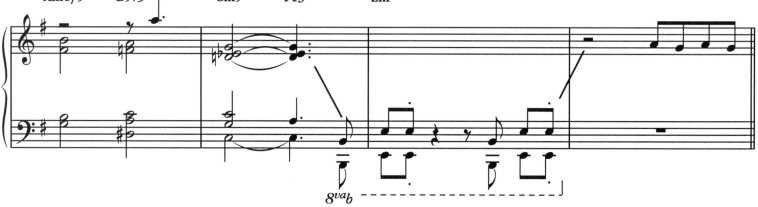

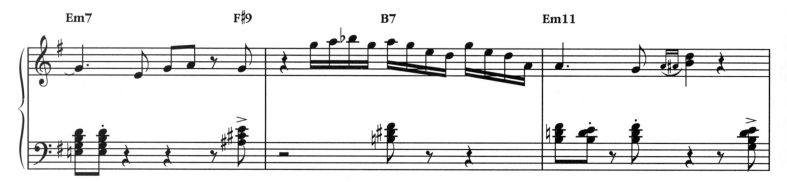

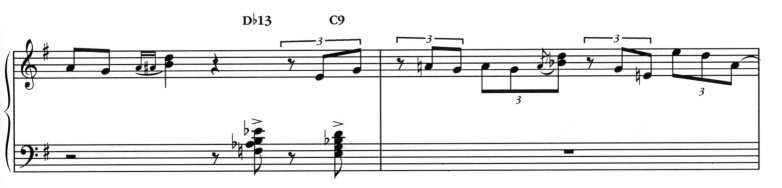

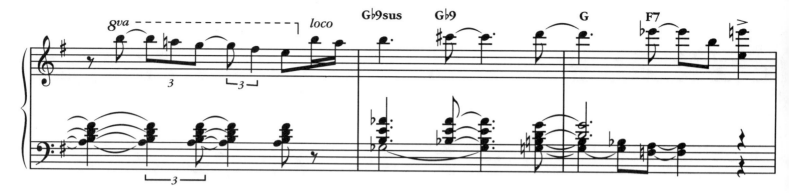

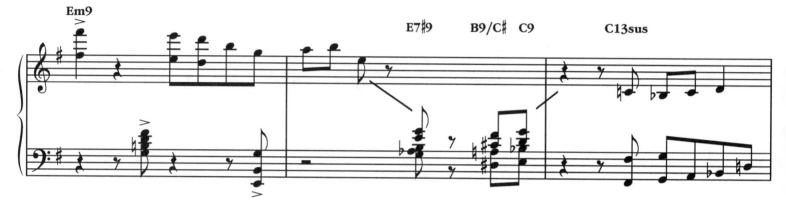

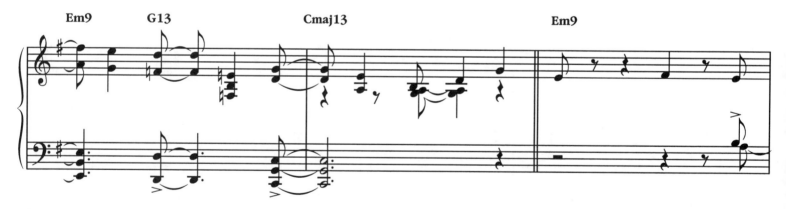

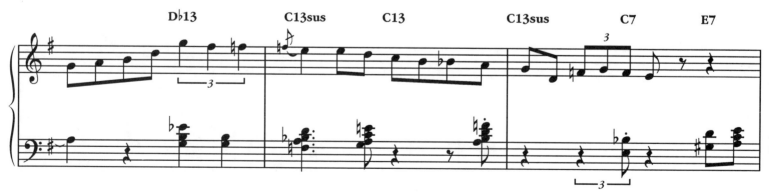

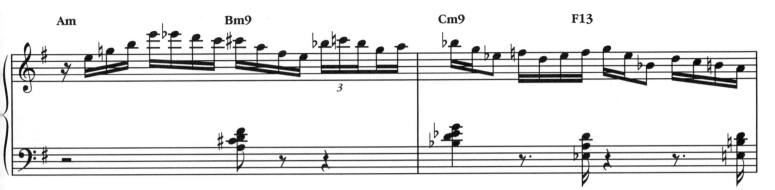

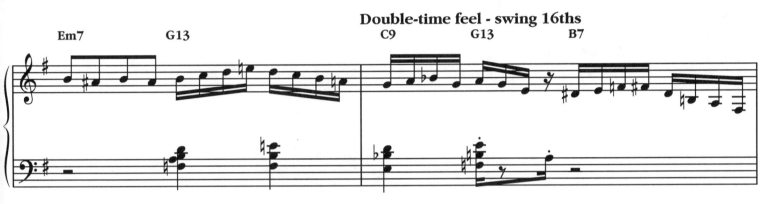

**Double-time feel - swing 16ths**

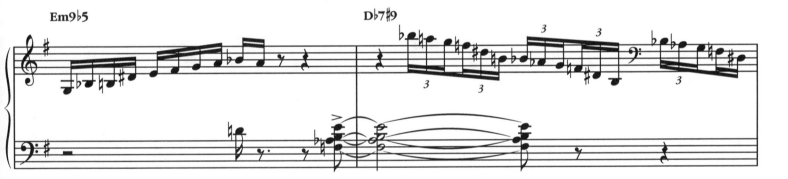

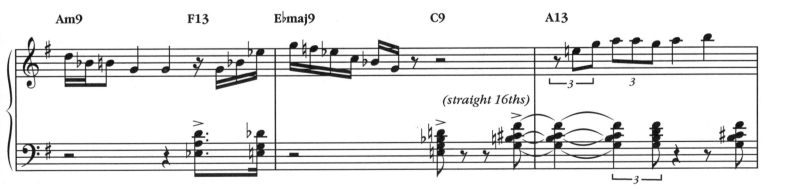

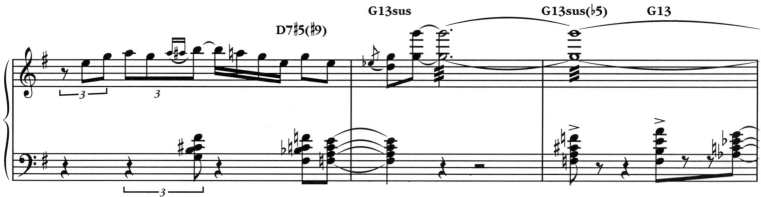

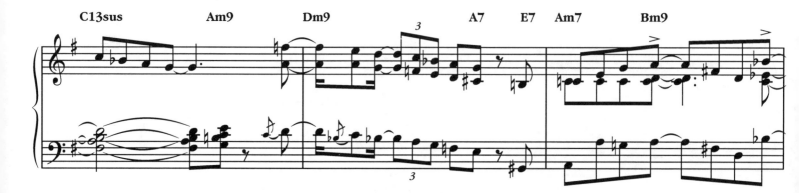

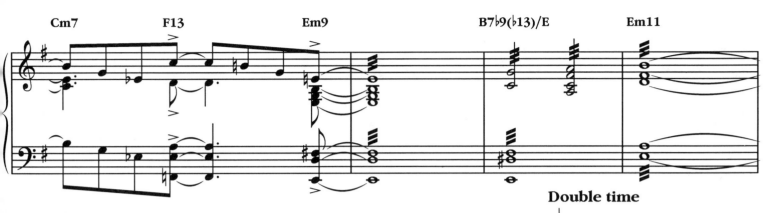

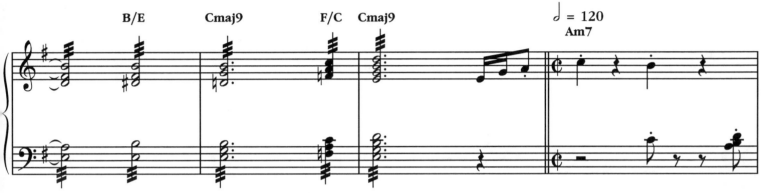

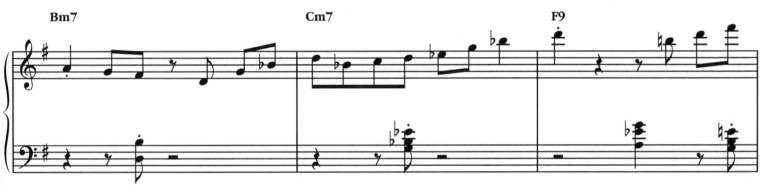

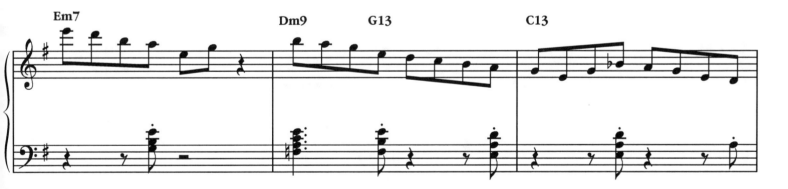

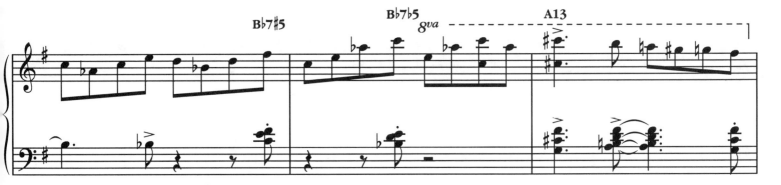

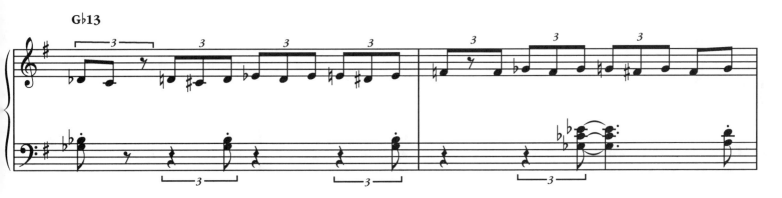

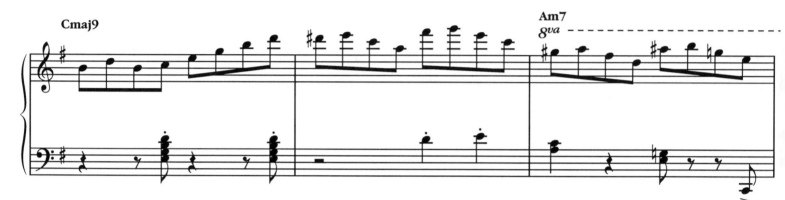

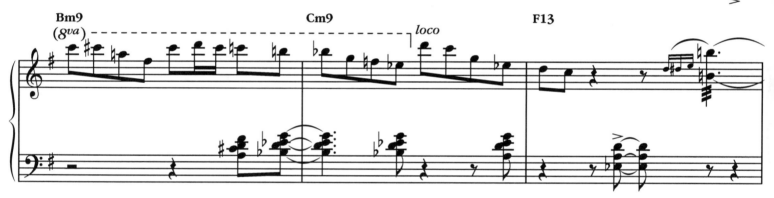

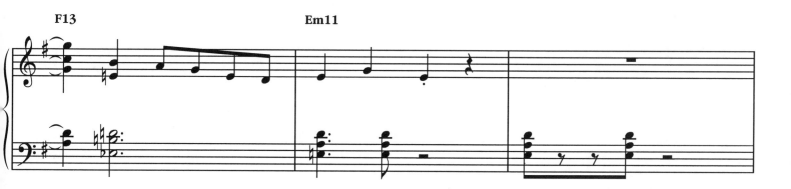

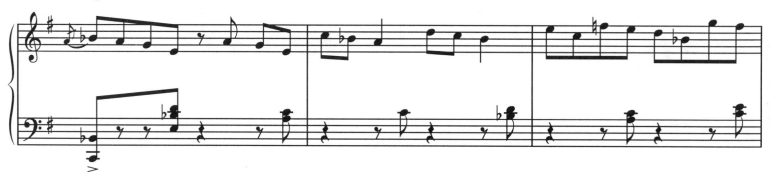

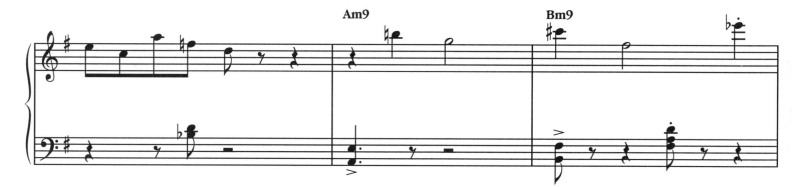

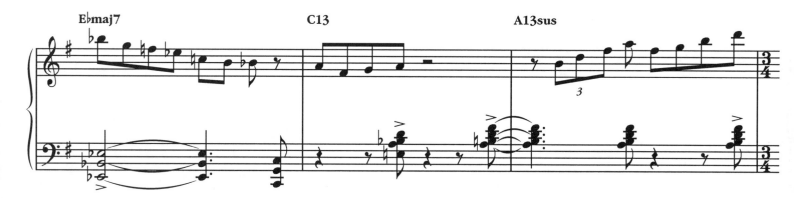

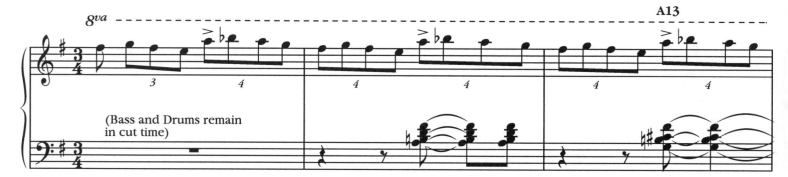

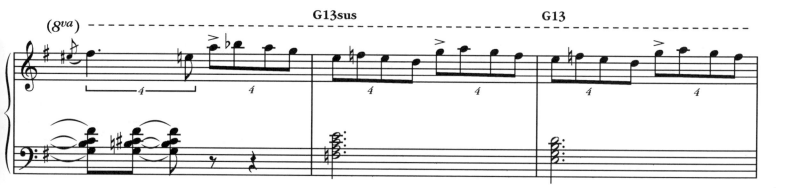

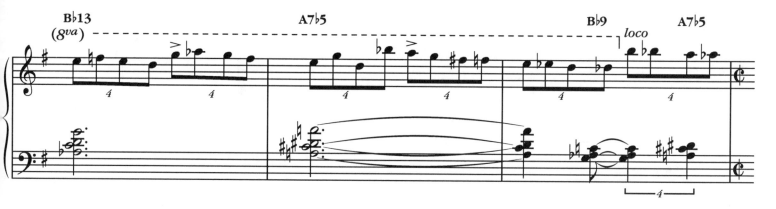

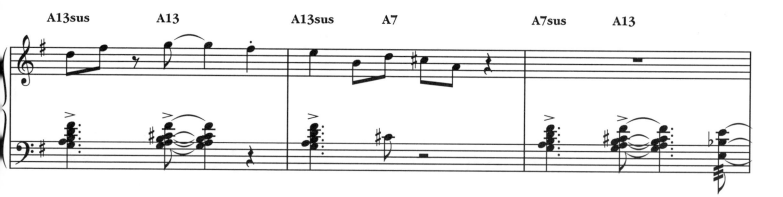

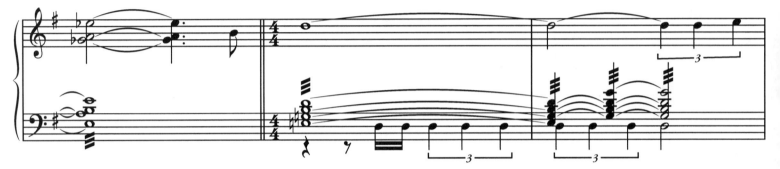

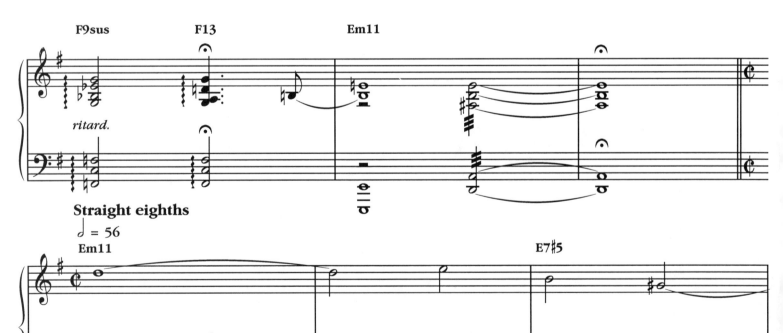

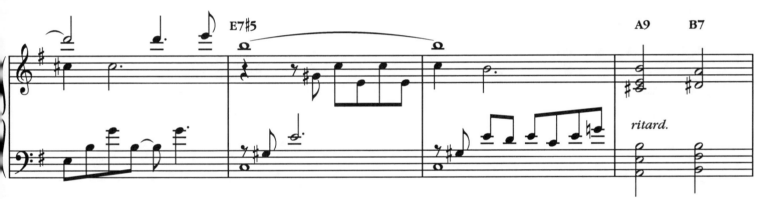

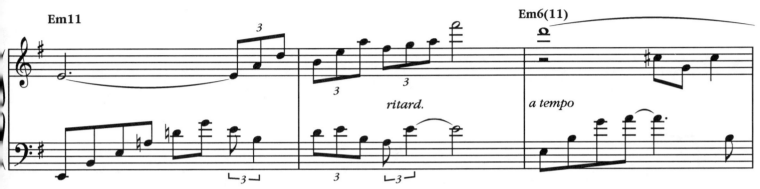

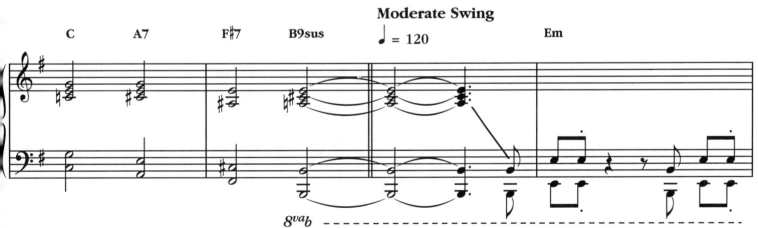

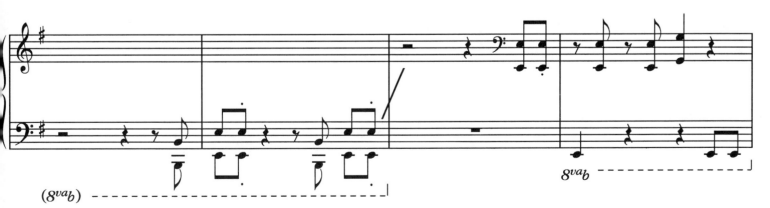

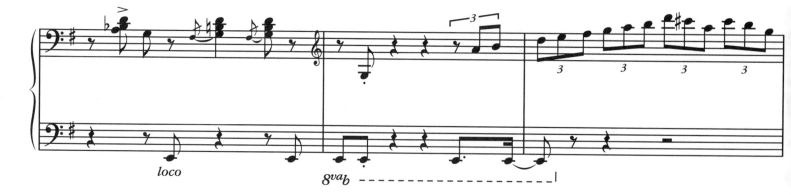

*loco*

*8va*<sub>b</sub>

*8va*<sub>b</sub>

*loco*

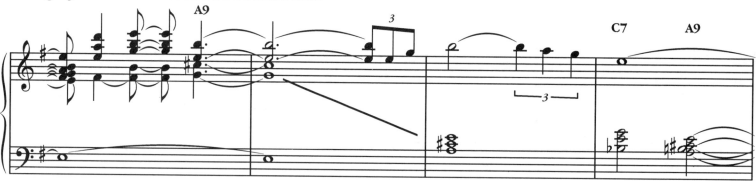

*8va*<sub>b</sub>

**A9**

**C7**    **A9**

**Em**

*8va*<sub>b</sub>

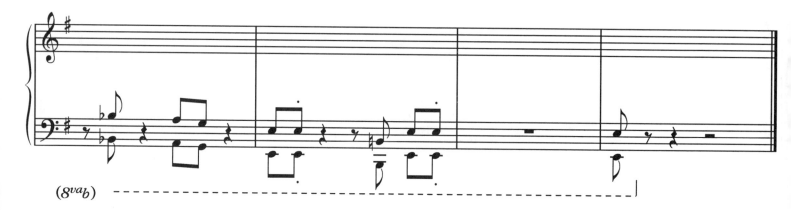

*(8va*<sub>b</sub>*)*

# ARTIST TRANSCRIPTIONS®

Artist Transcriptions are authentic, note-for-note transcriptions of the hottest artists in jazz, pop, and rock today. These outstanding, accurate arrangements are in an easy-to-read format which includes all essential lines. Artist Transcriptions can be used to perform, sequence or reference.

## Guitar & Bass

**The Guitar Book Of Pierre Bensusan**
00699072 .................................................... $19.95

**Ron Carter – Acoustic Bass**
00672331 .................................................... $16.95

**Charley Christian – The Art Of Jazz Guitar**
00026704 ...................................................... $6.95

**Stanley Clarke Collection**
00672307 .................................................... $19.95

**Larry Coryell – Jazz Guitar Solos**
00699140 ...................................................... $9.95

**Al Di Meola – Cielo E Terra**
00604041 .................................................... $14.95

**Al Di Meola – Friday Night In San Francisco**
00660115 .................................................... $14.95

**Al Di Meola – Music, Words, Pictures**
00604043 .................................................... $14.95

**Kevin Eubanks Guitar Collection**
00672319 .................................................... $19.95

**The Jazz Style Of Tal Farlow**
00673245 .................................................... $19.95

**Bela Fleck and the Flecktones**
00672359 Melody/Lyrics/Chords ........... $14.95

**David Friesen – Departure**
00673221 .................................................... $14.95

**David Friesen – Years Through Time**
00673253 .................................................... $14.95

**Frank Gambale**
00673223 .................................................... $19.95

**Best Of Frank Gambale**
00672336 .................................................... $19.95

**Jim Hall – Jazz Guitar Environments**
00699388 Book/Cassette .......................... $17.95
00699389 Book/CD ................................... $19.95

**Jim Hall – Exploring Jazz Guitar**
00699306 .................................................... $16.95

**Scott Henderson Guitar Book**
00699330 .................................................... $19.95

**Allan Holdsworth –
Reaching For The Uncommon Chord**
00604049 .................................................... $14.95

**Leo Kottke – Eight Songs**
00699215 .................................................... $14.95

**Wes Montgomery – Guitar Transcriptions**
00675536 .................................................... $14.95

**John Patitucci**
00673216 .................................................... $14.95

**Django Reinhardt Anthology**
00027083 .................................................... $14.95

**The Genius of Django Reinhardt**
00026711 .................................................... $10.95

**Django Reinhardt – A Treasury of Songs**
00026715 .................................................... $12.95

**John Renbourn – The Nine Maidens, The Hermit,
Stefan and John**
00699071 .................................................... $12.95

**Great Rockabilly Guitar Solos**
00692820 .................................................... $14.95

**John Scofield – Guitar Transcriptions**
00603390 .................................................... $16.95

**Segovia, Andres – 20 Studies For The Guitar**
00006362 Book/Cassette .......................... $14.95

**Mike Stern Guitar Book**
00673224 .................................................... $16.95

**Mark Whitfield**
00672320 .................................................... $19.95

**Jack Wilkins – Windows**
00673249 .................................................... $14.95

**Gary Willis Collection**
00672337 .................................................... $19.95

## Flute

**James Newton – Improvising Flute**
00660108 .................................................... $14.95

## Piano & Keyboard

**Monty Alexander Collection**
00672338 .................................................... $19.95

**Kenny Barron Collection**
00672318 .................................................... $22.95

**Warren Bernhardt Collection**
00672364 .................................................... $19.95

**Billy Childs Collection**
00673242 .................................................... $19.95

**Chick Corea – Beneath The Mask**
00673225 .................................................... $12.95

**Chick Corea – Inside Out**
00673209 .................................................... $12.95

**Chick Corea – Eye Of The Beholder**
00660007 .................................................... $14.95

**Chick Corea – Light Years**
00674305 .................................................... $14.95

**Chick Corea – Elektric Band**
00603126 .................................................... $15.95

**Chick Corea – Paint The World**
00672300 .................................................... $12.95

**Benny Green Collection**
00672329 .................................................... $19.95

**Ahmad Jamal Collection**
00672322 .................................................... $19.95

**Michel Petrucciani**
00673226 .................................................... $17.95

**Joe Sample – Ashes To Ashes**
00672310 .................................................... $14.95

**Horace Silver Collection**
00672303 .................................................... $19.95

**Art Tatum Collection**
00672316 .................................................... $22.95

**Billy Taylor Collection**
00672357 .................................................... $24.95

**McCoy Tyner**
00673215 .................................................... $14.95

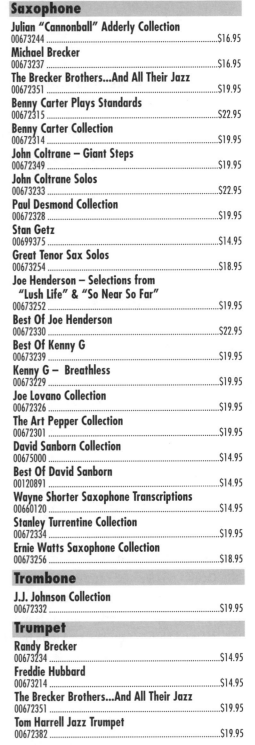

## Saxophone

**Julian "Cannonball" Adderly Collection**
00672344 .................................................... $16.95

**Michael Brecker**
00673237 .................................................... $16.95

**The Brecker Brothers...And All Their Jazz**
00672351 .................................................... $19.95

**Benny Carter Plays Standards**
00672315 .................................................... $22.95

**Benny Carter Collection**
00672314 .................................................... $19.95

**John Coltrane – Giant Steps**
00672349 .................................................... $19.95

**John Coltrane Solos**
00673233 .................................................... $22.95

**Paul Desmond Collection**
00672328 .................................................... $19.95

**Stan Getz**
00699375 .................................................... $14.95

**Great Tenor Sax Solos**
00673254 .................................................... $18.95

**Joe Henderson – Selections from
"Lush Life" & "So Near So Far"**
00673252 .................................................... $19.95

**Best Of Joe Henderson**
00672330 .................................................... $22.95

**Best Of Kenny G**
00672339 .................................................... $19.95

**Kenny G – Breathless**
00673229 .................................................... $19.95

**Joe Lovano Collection**
00672326 .................................................... $19.95

**The Art Pepper Collection**
00672301 .................................................... $19.95

**David Sanborn Collection**
00675000 .................................................... $14.95

**Best Of David Sanborn**
00120891 .................................................... $14.95

**Wayne Shorter Saxophone Transcriptions**
00660120 .................................................... $14.95

**Stanley Turrentine Collection**
00672334 .................................................... $19.95

**Ernie Watts Saxophone Collection**
00673256 .................................................... $18.95

## Trombone

**J.J. Johnson Collection**
00672332 .................................................... $19.95

## Trumpet

**Randy Brecker**
00673234 .................................................... $14.95

**Freddie Hubbard**
00673214 .................................................... $14.95

**The Brecker Brothers...And All Their Jazz**
00672351 .................................................... $19.95

**Tom Harrell Jazz Trumpet**
00672382 .................................................... $19.95

FOR MORE INFORMATION, SEE YOUR LOCAL MUSIC DEALER,
OR WRITE TO:

# HAL•LEONARD®
CORPORATION

7777 W. BLUEMOUND RD. P.O.BOX 13819 MILWAUKEE, WI 53213

Prices and availability subject to change without notice. Some products may not be available outside the U.S.A.

1297

# THE HAL LEONARD REAL JAZZ BOOK

## CHECK OUT THESE GREAT FEATURES!

- *Terrific songs in styles including standards, bebop, Latin, fusion & more!*

- *Lots of original material associated with major artists*

- *Hard-to-find modern jazz repertoire*

- *Many songs appearing in print for the first time ever!*

- *Lyrics are included if they exist for a tune*

- *Easy-to-read music typography*

- *A songwriter index for reference*

## OUTSTANDING JAZZ ARTISTS REPRESENTED INCLUDE:

Louis Armstrong • Count Basie • Bix Beiderbecke • Dave Brubeck • Billy Childs • Nat King Cole • John Coltrane • Chick Corea • Miles Davis • Al DiMeola • Billy Eckstine • Duke Ellington • Peter Erskine • Kevin Eubanks • Bill Evans • Ella Fitzgerald • Dizzy Gillespie • Benny Green • Dave Grusin • Herbie Hancock • Coleman Hawkins • Billie Holiday • Dick Hyman • Al Jarreau • Antonio Carlos Jobim • Thad Jones • Abbey Lincoln • Joe Lovano • Chuck Magione • Pat Metheny • Charles Mingus • Thelonious Monk • Jelly Roll Morton • Gerry Mulligan • Oliver Nelson • Charlie Parker • John Patitucci • Art Pepper • Oscar Peterson • Bud Powell • Django Reinhardt • The Rippingtons • Sonny Rollins • Horace Silver • Spyro Gyra • Steely Dan • Mike Stern • Art Tatum • McCoy Tyner • Sarah Vaughan • Fats Waller • Weather Report

*AND MANY MORE JAZZ GREATS!*

---

## OVER 500 SONGS, INCLUDING THESE GREAT STANDARDS:

Alfie • Alice in Wonderland • April in Paris • Autumn in New York • Besame Mucho • Black Coffee • Brazil • Caravan • Cast Your Fate to the Wind • Don't Worry 'Bout Me • (Meet) The Flintstones • Georgia on My Mind • Girl Talk • Gravy Waltz • How Deep Is the Ocean • I Wished on the Moon • I Got the World on a String • In a Sentimental Mood • In the Wee Small Hours of the Morning • Isn't It Romantic? • Jitterbug Waltz • Lover • Makin' Whoopee! • Mission: Impossible Theme • Mood Indigo • My Old Flame • Norwegian Wood • Out of Nowhere • The Rainbow Connection • The Shadow of Your Smile • Somebody Loves Me • Sophisticated Lady • Star Dust • Stella by Starlight • Take Five • Tangerine • This Masquerade • Too Late Now • The Very Thought of You • Watermelon Man • Wave • When Sunny Gets Blue • hundreds more!

FOR MORE INFORMATION, SEE YOUR LOCAL MUSIC DEALER, OR WRITE TO:

## HAL•LEONARD® CORPORATION

7777 W. BLUEMOUND RD. P.O. BOX 13819 MILWAUKEE, WI 53213

*Available in three editions:*

| | |
|---|---|
| 00240097 C Edition | $35.00 |
| 00240122 B♭ Edition | $35.00 |
| 00240123 E♭ Edition | $35.00 |

Price, contents, and availability subject to change without notice.